William Kay

Crisis Hupfeldiana

Being an examination of Hupfeld's criticism on Genesis, as recently set

forth in Bishop Colenso's Fifth part

William Kay

Crisis Hupfeldiana
Being an examination of Hupfeld's criticism on Genesis, as recently set forth in Bishop Colenso's Fifth part

ISBN/EAN: 9783337268404

Printed in Europe, USA, Canada, Australia, Japan

Cover: Foto ©Lupo / pixelio.de

More available books at **www.hansebooks.com**

CRISIS HUPFELDIANA;

BEING AN EXAMINATION OF

HUPFELD'S CRITICISM ON GENESIS,

AS RECENTLY SET FORTH IN

BISHOP COLENSO'S

FIFTH PART.

BY

W. KAY, D.D.,

FELLOW OF LINCOLN COLLEGE, OXFORD;
AND PRINCIPAL OF BISHOP'S COLLEGE, CALCUTTA.

"And Isaac dug again the wells of water which had been digged in the days of Abraham his father; for the Philistines had stopped them after Abraham's death; and he called their names after the names by which his father had called them."—*Gen.* xxvi. 18.

Oxford and London:
JOHN HENRY AND JAMES PARKER.
1865.

Printed by Messrs. Parker, Cornmarket, Oxford.

CONTENTS.

INTRODUCTION.

SECTION I.

ON THE USE MADE OF THE DIVINE NAMES IN THE ATTEMPTED DISINTEGRATION OF GENESIS.

                                                                                     PAGE

CHAP. I. On the Ideas to be associated with the Divine Names, ELOHIM and YAHVEH . . . 9

II. How the Divine Names are employed in Genesis . 13

III. On the right interpretation of Exod. vi. 2—8 . 18

IV. Failure of the attempt to employ the Divine Names as a Criterion of diverse Authorship . 21

SECTION II.

ON THE ATTEMPT TO MAKE OUT A DIVERSITY OF STYLE, WITH A VIEW TO THE DISMEMBERMENT OF GENESIS.

CHAP. I. The Character of the so-called Argument from "Style" 33

    APPENDIX. On Dr. Colenso's qualifications for conducting an Enquiry into Hebrew "Style" . 35

II. The Worth of the Phraseological Test . . 39

III. On the Way in which the Test is applied . . 43

    APPENDIX. On Ps. lxviii. 1 44

IV. The kind of Manipulation by which the "Analyst" gets at his Results 46

V. Consideration of two specially strong cases, pointed to by Dr. Colenso as irreconcileable with unity of Authorship 53

SECTION III.

THE REAL NATURE OF THE PRETENDED "ANALYSIS," VIEWED IN ITS PRINCIPLES, ITS METHOD, AND ITS RESULTS.

PAGE

CHAP. I. The Principles on which the Disintegration-theory rests:—(1) Religious Unbelief; (2) Historical Pyrrhonism 59

    APPENDIX. On Dr. Colenso's Translation of 'Oort on Baal-worship' 71

II. The Method by which the "Critics" support their foregone conclusions; viz. by introducing (1) Imaginary Cancellings; (2) Lacunæ; (3) Charges of Inadvertency. (4) Extreme Sub-division; (5) Arbitrary Assertions. 73

III. The Results of the "Analysis;"—(1) The 'Elohistic;' (2) The 'Jehovistic' Document . 80

CONCLUSION 91

INTRODUCTION.

THERE is a wide-spread opinion, at present, that learned Orientalists have made some discoveries about the "*style*" of Genesis, which seem to prove that the book could not have been written by Moses, or indeed by any *single* writer;—that it must, in fact, be considered (in Bishop COLENSO's words [a]) "a composite narrative, the work of several different authors, who lived *in different ages;*" or (as he says elsewhere [b]) "writing each from his own point of view *in very different ages.*"

Some few persons, who are equal to the task of examining the grounds of this opinion, have asserted that there is no foundation for it,—that it is "a mere toy, a mere exercise of fancy-criticism [c]." But, for the most part, our theologians have been content to rest their rejection of the supposed "critical" results on general, historical and religious, grounds; —the criticism meanwhile being left as *an unsolved difficulty*. Educated themselves in habits of sober and cautious philosophizing, English scholars have been unwilling to suppose that the criticism, which was put forth so confidently, and received so submissively, abroad, rested on no solid grounds whatever.

Dean MILMAN supplies an interesting illustration of this state of mind. His historical training enables him to say: "The internal evidence .... in the Mosaic records is to me conclusive. *All attempts to assign a later period for the author-*

---

[a] *The Pentateuch and Book of Joshua critically examined: Part* V: p. 305.
[b] *Ib.*, p. 43.   [c] *Quarterly Review:* April, 1863: p. 486.

ship, or even for the compilation, though made by scholars of the highest ability, are so irreconcileable with facts, so self-destructive, and so mutually destructive, that *I acquiesce without hesitation in their general antiquity*[d]." Again; after speaking affectionately of his friend Baron BUNSEN, he says of him[e]: "He seems to me to labour under the same too common infirmity, the passion for making history without historical materials. *In this conjectural history, founded on conjectural grounds, he is as positive and peremptory* (they often differ) *as Ewald himself.* I confess that I have not much sympathy for this—not, making bricks without straw, but—*making bricks entirely of straw, and offering them as solid materials.*"

So far all is clear. He is in his own province, and sees his way. But, when he refers to the philological question, he adopts an entirely different tone. "There may," he says[f], "be some certain discernible marks and signs of difference in age and authorship. *But that any critical microscope, in the nineteenth century, can be so exquisite and so powerful as to dissect the whole with perfect nicety,* to decompose it, and assign each separate paragraph to its special origin in three, four, or five, or more, independent documents, ... this seems to me a task which *no mastery of the Hebrew language, with all its kindred tongues, no discernment, however fine and discriminating, can achieve.*" Again, after allowing its weight to "the argument from language[g]," as resting upon "the introduction of new words, of words used in new senses, of new

[d] *History of the Jews:* vol. i. p. 45, 6. Cp. p. 132. "An adversary of such opinions might almost stand aloof in calm patience, and *leave the conflicting theorists to mutual slaughter.*"

[e] p. xxiv, xxv. May I presume to express a hope that the venerable writer may yet be enabled to disengage himself *wholly* from the "Rationalists," whose irrationalism he has so well pointed out in many parts of his Third Edition? There are still some passages in his book which can only be read with surprise and regret. This, however, makes his testimony the more valuable where he is right.

[f] p. xxiii.   [g] p. 133.

forms, new grammatical constructions," &c., he adds, that such instruments " must be applied *with the finest observation, with the most exquisite and suspicious nicety.*" Again: " There may, no doubt, be niceties both of style and language *to be detected by fine critical sagacity, by exquisite judgment, by long and patient study* [h]." And once more, he speaks of "*those slight changes of phrases and words which are discerned with such exquisite and subtle knowledge and ingenuity* by the scholars of our day [i]."

This is all extremely interesting, as shewing what an English scholar would naturally *expect* to be the qualifications of men who undertook the task of "analyzing" the book of Genesis. As applied, however, to the actual process carried on by the "Critics," such observations are the *severest irony;*—the more cutting, because made in entire unconsciousness of their effect. The philology of the neo-critics is, at least, as conjectural and arbitrary as the history of Baron Bunsen. Much of it (the reader of the following pages will be able to judge for himself) is inexpressibly puerile.

Perhaps some apology may be needed for my having taken Dr. Colenso's Book as the subject of review in these pages, and not that of his leader, Professor HUPFELD [k]. The reasons for adopting such a course are sufficiently obvious. Not one in ten thousand would be able to verify my references to

---

[h] p. 135.   [i] p. 209.

[k] "*Die Quellen der Genesis und die Art ihrer Zusammensetzung.*" (Berlin: 1853.) At p. vi of his "*Vorrede*" Prof. Hupfeld speaks of "the TRUSTFULNESS, which an Inquirer and Guide into the regions of the *higher Criticism* finds it *indispensable* to demand from his readers; especially," he says, "in our crafty (*abgefeimten*) times, when men have learnt so cleverly, like the Sophists of Greece, *to defend what is most perverse, to distort what is most simple, and to make anything out of anything.*" Certainly he has no reason to complain of Dr. Colenso on the ground of *want of trustfulness*. Even when Dr. Colenso differs from Hupfeld, it is *on Hupfeldian grounds.*

Hupfeld; all who will, may readily have access to Dr. Colenso's publication. The German Professor's speculation might have been safely left to be dealt with by German theologians; Dr. Colenso's comes before the public with an emphatic statement that it is considered by its author to be "THE MOST IMPORTANT PART" of his notorious attack on the Pentateuch [1].

I have undertaken the task with reluctance, on many accounts.

1. The whole book, 688 pages thick, is so full of coarse insinuation against the writers of Holy Scripture, and so destitute of critical taste, of historical perception, and, above all, of reverence for Divine things, that it is painful to read it at all, much more, therefore, to examine it in detail. One is inclined to say, "Is it not better to leave *him* with the whole responsibility of whatever harm his books may do, and not to run the risk of *spreading* the evil by repeating, though it be in order to refute, his errors?"

2. The very refutation of this theory makes it necessary to use terms, which of themselves involve the erroneous theory, and which, besides, can scarcely be used, as they are by the critics, without profaneness:—I mean, the words "Jehovist" and "Elohist."

To employ these terms is, at once, to concede standing-ground to a perfectly gratuitous theory. What then must be the effect of scattering these terms over hundreds of pages as thickly as x's and y's are spread over a book of algebra? Nor is the unfair effect of this on the argument the only injurious result; a still worse consequence is its obvious tendency to deaden the feeling of reverence which ought

---

[1] *Pref.*, p. xliv. "I send forth my Fifth Part into the world, content with knowing that this volume contains *the most important part of my work*, so that if, in God's Providence, I should be prevented from completing it, I shall have at least carried it so far as *to secure the main object of my labours*."

ever to attach to the "glorious and aweful Name [m]" of GOD Most High.

Voltaire once acknowledged to Dr. Clarke how much he had been impressed with Sir Isaac Newton's habit of never uttering the name of GOD without a slight *pause*,—as if for self-recollection. What religious mind does not wish ever to feel thus? How else, indeed, can we truly pray, (the very first petition of the Lord's Prayer,) "HALLOWED BE THY NAME"?

3. The inanity of the pretended arguments is such, that, for the most part, there is nothing in them capable of sustaining an argumentative blow;—it is like beating the air. The "critics" abstain from stating what their *principles of reasoning* are, and assume their *facts* without evidence. One is reminded of the old task of binding Proteus. Shew that they have overlooked a fact which is plainly at variance with their statements;—at once they re-adjust their assertions, (with the most lavish prodigality of hypothesis,) so as to include this once adverse fact within their lines. How could you refute an adherent of the old Ptolemaic system of astronomy, who persisted in adding-on a new "epicycle" to account for every fresh astronomical fact which you brought forward? Only the absurd complication of his theory could at last bring him to adopt the simple notion of a Central Force, in exchange for his unlimited supply of (imaginary) celestial mechanism.

It is my hope that this small pamphlet may suggest to some,—and may Bishop Colenso be among the number!—how all the facts, which are so unintelligible on their scheme of gratuitous assumptions, readily fall into order and harmony, when the true view of the sacred names is adopted.

Let me add, however, that these pages will be chiefly

[m] Deut. xxviii. 58.

engaged with the refutation of errors. I hope to speak more largely on the positive value of the Divine Names in another place. My chief object here will be *to exhibit the hollowness of the claims put forth by the self-styled 'Criticism;'* —the larger part of the evidence being drawn from *the 'Critics' themselves.*

It is difficult to carry on a work of this kind, without appearing sometimes to bear hardly on the individual whose writings are the subject of comment. It is my earnest desire to avoid to the utmost anything which (however true) may irritate rather than convince. Even in my own mind I pass no judgment on the motives of men like Bishop Colenso and Professor Hupfeld. I am utterly at a loss how to explain the fact that they should have been deluded, (as they appear to be,) by the transparent sophisms, the arbitrary suppositions, the flagrant violations of all historical probability, which abound in their writings. Had the books related to mere abstract science or literature, one might have been content to employ the expression that was used of Pére Hardouin's writings,—"ses livres *ont perdu le droit d'être refutés.*" But though the *books* have forfeited all claim to be answered, the Church and the world have not forfeited their right of asking that extravagances on so momentous a subject should not pass down the stream of time unexposed.

That even their mistakes shall be overruled to good, I doubt not. Many a plant has been fructified by means of pollen which was brought to it unwittingly by an insect intent solely on plans of its own:—and even a vagrant scepticism, bent only on accomplishing a work of destruction, may turn out to have been instrumental in fecundating theological science.

SECTION I.

ON THE USE MADE OF THE DIVINE NAMES
אלהים AND יהוה,
IN THE ATTEMPTED DISINTEGRATION OF
GENESIS.

"Man würde vielmehr sich über diesen auffallenden Misgriff und Rückfall der neuesten Kritik wundern dürfen, ... wenn man nicht die tyrannische Macht kännte die eine herrschende Richtung oder angenommene Theorie unbewust über den Geist auch der Besseren ausübt."

(HUPFELD, Die Quellen, p. 77.)

CHAPTER I.

On the Ideas to be associated with the Divine Names ELOHIM and YAHVEH, (commonly read, JEHOVAH).

1. THE distinction between the two names is in general quite obvious. E.g., in that oft-recurring phrase, "I am YAHVEH, your Elohim," it is clear that we could no more transpose the two words, than in the expression, "I am Joseph, your brother," we could interchange the words "Joseph" and "brother." '*Yahveh*' stands as the *personal* name of the Being who is speaking; while 'Elohim' is in the nature of a common noun, (though there be but One, in fact, who can be connoted by it).

2. More particularly; ELOHIM expressed the character of Him "whose Eternal Power and Godhead[a]," discerned in the works of nature, are objects of religious reverence[b] to man's spirit. YAHVEH, though etymologically signifying "self-existent," yet, as being the *personal* name, gathered up into association with itself whatever attributes were manifested in God's condescending intercourse with men, —especially, therefore, His righteousness, faithfulness, and mercy.

3. In this way provision was made, from the first, for the maintenance of a pure and true theology among the Israelites. The name ELOHIM (plural in form, yet actually singular) was adapted to be a protest against *polytheistic* views; —in Him, the one God, all Divine Powers co-existed. Yet not as *Pantheism* sums up the forces of the Universe into one; for (said the name YAHVEH) He is a *Personal* God.

---

[a] Rom. i. 20.   [b] The word is probably derived from a root which survives in Arabic as *alīha*, to fear.

And that this Personal Being was not "a God afar off," in the depths of Infinite space or of Absolute existence, was further ascertained by the words, "I am YAHVEH, *thy God;*"—'who have placed myself in a special and condescending relation to *thee*.'

Here, I say, was provision made for a far deeper apprehension of the Divine character than any which unaided Reason, outside the circle of special Revelation, could possibly attain to.

4. To illustrate this let me quote a passage from the work of a recent thoughtful writer, who is meditating on "*the Ways of God, in connexion with Providence and Redemption*[c]," without the slightest reference to the fact upon which we are now intent. He says: "In this high and holy sphere of MORAL Government, there must be results unattainable by the exercise of *one* Divine perfection, or *by Power alone;* and which would make it needful (to speak with reverence) *that the High and Lofty One, who inhabits Eternity, should unbosom the secrets of His heart,* and unfold all the rich diversity of His heavenly goodness, His patient long-suffering, His stern severity and deep compassion, before the view of the wondering universe." Here we have philosophical speculation demanding that very distinction, for which the two Divine names in Hebrew have made provision. The general idea of Power, attached to ELOHIM, the Ruler of the universe, is not sufficient. There are infinite depths in the Divine Nature, which can only be known as manifested in the *personal* dealings of God with man. That God *would* hold intercourse with man was guaranteed by the existence of the personal name, YAHVEH.

5. That a very special revelation of God's character was eventually made in connexion with this name, is undeniable;—witness that well-known passage, Exod. xxxiv. 5—7; witness the great appellation, "Yahveh, *our Righteousness*[d];"

---

[c] MR. BIRKS: at p. 19 of a work having the above title.
[d] Jer. xxiii. 6.

witness (I may add) the whole Law, and Psalms, and Prophets.

6. This peculiarity of Israelitic theology,—its sense of God as a *gracious* Being, *in communion* with man,—is a plain matter of historical fact.

Let me appeal to one or two unsuspected witnesses.

Dean Milman says[e]: "In all this early narrative, [Gen. xii—xv,] the remarkable part is the conception of the Deity:—I. His Unity, His Almightiness..... II. His Immateriality. III. His *Personality, His active Personality. He is more than a Power, a Force, a Law*; He is a Being with a will, *with moral attributes, revealing Himself* more or less distinctly, and holding communication *not only as an overruling influence on material things, but with the inward consciousness of man.*" In writing thus, the historian had not the most distant notion of illustrating the use of the Sacred Names; but if he had been writing expressly with this view, he could scarcely have furnished a better exposition of the intention of the use of '*Elohim*' in Gen. i. and ii. 1—3, and of 'Yahveh-Elohim' in ii. 4, ff.

Similarly Professor Jowett remarks[f]: "*The wonders of Creation* are not ornaments or poetical figures strewed over the pages of the Old Testament by the hand of the artist, but the frame in which it consists. And yet *in this material garb the moral and spiritual nature of God is never lost sight of*. . . . The terrible imagery in which the Psalmist delights to array *His power*, is not inconsistent with *the gentlest feelings of love and trust*, such as are also expressed in the passage just now quoted, 'I will love Thee, O LORD, my strength.' God is in nature, because He is near also to the cry of His servants. The heart of man expands in His presence; he fears to die lest he should be taken from it. *There is nothing like this in any other religion in the world.* No Greek or Roman ever had the consciousness of love towards his God. No other sacred books can show a passage displaying such a range of

[e] *Hist. of Jews:* i. p. 13.   [f] St. Paul's Epp., ii. p. 451.

feeling as the eighteenth or the twenty-ninth Psalm,—*so awful a conception of the* MAJESTY OF GOD, *so true and tender a sense of* HIS RIGHTEOUSNESS AND LOVING-KINDNESS."

7. Here then that remarkable fact,—the existence of the two Sacred Names,—has an explanation; which is not only in itself simple and consistent, but also proved, by the testimony of unimpeachable witnesses, to have a *vera causa* corresponding to it.

8. There is absolutely nothing on the other side to set against this. "Criticism" cannot give any tolerable reply to this first question;—" How is it that prophets and saints were moved with such deep reverence and love for God's Holy Name? Why were they so zealous in praying that His Name might be known over all the earth? Why did they look on this knowledge as so very precious?" To the " critics" the variation of the Sacred Names is, for the most part, a matter of mere arbitrary caprice, or accident. How, indeed, *could* they embrace the truth, when that truth is diametrically opposed to the Unbelief on which their pseudo-criticism has taken its stand? Having persuaded themselves that there is no *personal intervention of God* possible, they can but hasten to annihilate the testimony to that intervention, which is borne by the use of the very name '*Yahveh*' in the sacred writings.

What remains but that they obtrude upon us the fictitious hypothesis of two authors (or sets of authors) studiously attaching themselves, (no one can say why,) to mere *names as such*,—empty and formal distinctions, from which all life has fled?—that they drag us through a weary, meaningless, complication of verbal details, which depend on no principle, and lead to no end;—the driest and most meagre verbal speculations the world has ever seen? Who, that has looked at their pretended " Analysis," does not feel that they are in want of that *appropriate conception*[g], which alone can reduce the facts to intelligible unity?

[g] See Dr. Whewell's *Phil. of the Ind. Sc.*, Bk. xi.

CHAP. II.] *Reverence of God's Name a first principle.*   13

9. Let me add, that these Sacred Names are everywhere in Scripture referred to with deepest reverence. One of the Commandments of the First Table of the Law is directed against a light use of the Name. The very purpose of the Law is summed up thus: "*that thou mayest fear this glorious and aweful name,* YAHTEH, *thy God* [h]." This reverence continued to be the badge of true religion down to the latest times: "*A book of remembrance was written before Him for them that feared* YAHTEH, *and that thought upon His* NAME." We may unhesitatingly affirm that any theory, which neglects (much more, which systematically offends against) these first principles of Jewish piety,—which treats the Sacred Names as it might treat algebraic formulæ,—cannot be a true one. It is αὐτοκατάκριτος, self-condemned.

CHAPTER II.

How the Divine Names are employed in Genesis.

1. CRITICISM *assumes* that the use of the two Divine Names indicates a difference of authorship [i].

Our previous chapter has shewn that such an assumption is groundless; since the distinction of names corresponds to *a real distinction of ideas*. We now proceed briefly to shew, by a few instances, that the facts of the case are in harmony with the explanation we have given.

The reader will bear in mind that the instances here produced are only intended to *exemplify* what has been said. A full discussion of the use of the Divine Names in Holy Scripture (a very fruitful subject) is not needed, or indeed suited, for our present purpose.

2. We can scarcely have a better illustration of the whole

---

[h] Deut. xxviii. 58.

[i] This assumption was made originally on the strength of a misinterpretation of Exod. vi. 2—8: (on which see the next Chap.).

question than is supplied by the first four chapters of Genesis.

(*a*) In Chap. i and ii. 1—3, the name ELOHIM is used throughout:—for in it we have the exercise of that Divine Power, Wisdom, and Goodness, of which Heaven and Earth have been preaching to man ever since he first drew breath.

(*b*) In chap. iv, when man has "fallen short of the glory of GOD[k]," and can only be restored to it by the intervention of Divine Mercy, working out that long process of redemption and moral discipline in the midst of which we ourselves are still living, the name YAHVEH is employed. In this Name "mercy and judgment" are combined; whilst God, in great condescension coming near to the first human family, accepts righteous Abel, warns and judges Cain.

(*c*) In the intermediate Section (ii. 4, ... iii.) we have the two names *conjoined*, (*twenty* times;—there is only one other place in the Pentateuch where this conjunction occurs, viz. Exod. ix. 30.) The introduction of the name YAHVEH corresponds to the advance made in the narrative[1]; which no longer exhibits man as standing amidst the works of Creation, but views him as a moral being, placed in a special relation to God as a loving Father, whose command he is bound by every tie of gratitude to obey.

(*d*) Just so in Ps. xix, the Sacred Name "EL" is used in the First Part, (*vv.* 1—6), of which the sum is, "The heavens declare the glory of GOD;"—whilst the Second Part, beginning, "The law of the LORD is perfect," has only the name "YAHVEH," (*seven* times.)

(*e*) But whilst the use of the name YAHVEH indicates this advance, the name ELOHIM, employed in the former Chapter, is retained *in combination with it;*—stamping for ever the correlation of the Two Names. He who is the gracious

---

[k] Rom. iii. 23.

[1] The change of Name was observed by Tertullian, *adv. Hermog.* c. 3, and by St. Augustine, *de Gen. ad lit.* viii. 2: (quoted by Hengstenberg, *Auth. d. Pent.* i. 181 ff.)

Saviour and Judge of men is none other than the Creator and Sustainer of the universe. Man's sin may, for awhile, require a severance between the Two Names. But Holy Scripture points to a time when the two shall be re-united, and all shall confess that "*The* LORD GOD *Omnipotent reigneth* ᵐ."

(*f*) Inside the Section ii. 4, . . . iii., however, we have a very instructive *variation* of the Name. In iii. 1—6, when the Tempter is conversing with Eve, the name 'Elohim' is used. "Yea, hath GOD said?" The *more remote* name was certainly well suited to his purpose. It altered the *point of view*. It suggested some such train of thought as this: "What? the *great Creator* care for your eating or not eating? He who made all things good, — can He have bidden you to abstain from what is good for food?" In other words, it removed the question away from the *moral*, to a speculative, rationalizing, point of view : — and how much was gained when that step was once taken!

3. In chap. v, (which, after reverting to the creation of man, traces the descent of Noah from Adam,) the name 'ELOHIM' is again employed. The propriety of this scarcely needs to be pointed out. But at ver. 29 of this chapter, where allusion is made to the curse which had fallen on the ground for man's sin, 'YAHVEH' recurs. That sentence had all along been a mark of God's *righteous intolerance of sin*. Rather than leave sin unpunished, He will have the spread of physical beauty and fertility over the earth arrested. Paradise shall remain for the present an unprolific germ. The ground at large shall be cursed;—in order that MAN may know that "it is an evil and a bitter thing *to forsake* THE LORD ⁿ."

4. In the middle of chap. v we are told that Enoch "walked with GOD:" and the same is said of Noah in vi. 9. On this latter passage it has been asked : "Why should it be in ver. 8, 'Noah found grace in the eyes of THE LORD,'

ᵐ Rev. xi. 17.   ⁿ Jer. ii. 19.

and yet in ver. 9, 'Noah walked with GOD?' *Why not rather,* '*walked with the Lord?*'"

The answer is easy. When God condescends to *accept* His servant, 'YAHVEH,' the Name of gracious condescension, is the appropriate term. When Noah rises into *the Divine life,* conformed more and more to "the image of *Him who created him,*" 'GOD' is the appropriate word.—For a like reason, we find always, "a man of God," "sons of God," (never, "a man of the Lord," or "sons of the Lord.")

5. Thus much in general may suffice for our present purpose. Any one who will pursue the inquiry may find abundance of evidence confirmatory of the distinction we have drawn.

Let it be observed, however, that, because it is fitting in certain cases that one or other of the Names should be used almost exclusively, it by no means follows that in other cases they may not *both* be employed in the same chapter, section, or even verse, according to the varying aspects of the subject-matter. It is the "same God, who works all in all;"—but it is as the Righteous One that He condemns the ante-diluvian race to death; as the Almighty that He executes the sentence. As God, He bids the waves of the sea roll in upon the land—so suspending for the time His own formative fiat, (Gen. i. 9, 10) ; as Lord, He bids Noah enter the ark, and closes the door behind him;—so setting the seal of His faithful love upon that floating sepulchre.

Again, it is no less obvious that there may be cases in which no *special* attention is called to this or that aspect of the Divine procedure; and therefore (since one name *must* be used) a very slight *inclination* of meaning would suffice in such instances to determine which should be employed.

For the most part, the appropriateness of the Name which actually occurs is readily seen.

6. Before closing this chapter, I must advert very briefly to one more portion of the Book of Genesis;—the History of Joseph, (chap. xxxvii, xxxix . . . l.) In this long portion

the name *Yahveh* occurs only in ch. xxxix and xlix. In ch. xxxix, indeed, it is used *eight times;* shedding its light over the captivity and imprisonment of Joseph. "The LORD was with Joseph and shewed him mercy." By means of that prolonged suffering the gracious YAHVEH was working out (not only Joseph's own spiritual discipline º, but also) an important step in the developement of the Covenant-promise.

After that, it might have seemed as if all went on by natural causes, under God's ordinary providential government:—as if the Covenant of special mercy, with its guarantee of Canaan, had withdrawn into the background, though the general power and wisdom and goodness of God stood out strongly to view. Accordingly ELOHIM is the word which is (with one exception, xlix. 18,) exclusively used in chh. xl—l.

In the midst of all this, however, the promise was not really forgotten. Jacob, dying at a distance from Canaan, parts the land among his twelve sons; and in the very centre of his dying Address records, in one brief sentence, what was at the core of his spiritual life. "I have waited for Thy salvation, O YAHVEH!"

Not God's wondrous *providential* Goodness,—but His *covenanted* Faithfulness,—was what the Patriarch's inmost soul relied upon.

7. These instances may suffice for shewing that the explanation given in the preceding chapter is not only (as was there seen) a *vera causa*, but is also an *adequate* cause. It explains the facts and throws light on the whole course of the narrative.

We have seen, too, that at the very outset of human history the Divine Names were used in conjunction; almost as if it had been intended to exclude any supposition of antagonism between them P.

º Of which the Psalm speaks (cv. 19), "The word (*or*, promise) of THE LORD *tried* him."

P So much even the Dismemberers are compelled to allow. See Colenso, p. 193; and *C. A.*, § 3. i.

8. There certainly, then, is no *primâ facie* reason, *internal to the book* itself, why from the employment of these two Divine Names any one should infer diversity of authorship. Quite the contrary. So harmonious a use of the Names helps to bind the whole book into indissoluble unity.

CHAPTER III.
On the right interpretation of Exod. vi. 2—8.

"WHENCE, then," it may be asked, "did the notion of inferring a diversity of authorship from the use of the two Divine Names take its rise?"

The whole process had its origin, notoriously, in a certain interpretation put upon Exod. vi. 2—8.

We must, therefore, say a few words on this question.

2. The chief cause of the mistake has been, want of attention to the meaning of the Hebrew verb נוֹדַע.

The exact rendering of the passage is; "God spake unto Moses and said, I am Yahveh: And I appeared to Abraham, to Isaac, and to Jacob in (quality of, *or* as [q]) God Almighty: and (in regard to) my name Yahveh I made not myself known [r] (נוֹדַעְתִּי) to them." The patriarchs had lived under the guardian care of the Almighty; but, as regarded the special name of covenanted Mercy, God had not *manifested in act* what He had promised.

That this actual manifestation of Himself by *experiential proof* is signified by נודע is made perfectly certain by such passages as the following:—

Ps. lxxvi. 1. "*Known* (נוֹדָע) in Judah is God; In Israel great is *His Name*:"—the reason of which is given in the remainder of the Psalm. He "had arisen to judgement, to

---

[q] Cf. the use of the French *en*.
[r] So the Eng. Ver. translates the word in Ezek. xx. 5, 9.

help all the meek ones of earth." He had manifested Himself *by facts*.

Ps. xlviii. "God in her palaces is known [s] (*or*, ascertained) as a fortress. FOR lo! the Kings assembled,—and were dismayed—and fled." This sense of the word may be almost said to be formulized in Ps. ix. 17. "KNOWN (נוֹדָע) is the LORD; *He has executed judgement*."

These passages shew that the verb denotes, not the communication of a new name, but the *making good in fact that which had previously been associated with the Name*.

This interpretation is all but expressly put into our hands by the prophet Ezekiel (xx. 9): "I wrought *for My Name's sake*, that it might not be polluted in the sight of the heathen, among whom they were; in whose sight *I made Myself known* (נוֹדַעְתִּי) to them, IN BRINGING THEM FORTH out of the land of Egypt."

With so express a comment, by a canonical writer, on the history of Exodus, there ought to be no further controversy as to the meaning of נוֹדַע.

3. *The whole context, moreover, requires this sense.* When Moses was bidden (Exod. iii. 15, 16) to go and say to the children of Israel, "*YAHVEH, the God of your fathers*, the God of Abraham, Isaac, and Jacob, has appeared to me:" he answered, "Lo, they will not give credence to me, nor hearken to my voice; *for they will say*, Yahveh has not appeared to thee." It never occurred to him that the people might say, "Who is Yahveh?—We never heard of such a name. Our fathers never told us of any such name. Why think to comfort us, under our overwhelming sorrows, by bringing us a strange, unheard-of, *name*?" His fear was,

---

[s] יָדַע. Cp. Exod. xxxiii. 16, "Whereby shall it be *ascertained* (יִוָּדַע) that I and Thy people have found grace in Thy sight?" And in Elijah's prayer, (1 Kings xviii. 36); "O YAHVEH, God of Abraham, Isaac, and Israel, let it be ascertained (and prove I by plain facts, יִוָּדַע) that Thou art GOD in Israel."

lest they should not believe that *the Person so designated* had communicated with him.

To meet this fear, Moses was empowered to work miracles (iv. 5,) "in order that they may believe that YAHVEH, *the God of their fathers*, the God of Abraham, Isaac, and Jacob, has appeared to thee."

When Moses's first visit to Pharaoh issued only in adding to their misery, they say: "YAHVEH look upon you and judge." They use His name naturally as one they were acquainted with; but they believe that Moses had not really received a message from Him. To remedy this incredulity was the purpose of the assurance given in vi. 2—8. It begins with " I am Yahveh ;" just as when Joseph made himself known to his brethren he began with, " I am Joseph." In both cases, it was the re-appearance of a *person ;* who, though intimately known of old to the parties addressed, had for a long time not held (or seemed not to be holding) any communication with them. The burden of the address was, —that He was now about *to fulfil the promise* which He had made to their fathers; " And *ye shall know that I am* YAHVEH *your God.*"

Most assuredly the consolation conveyed in this message did not lie in the *promulgation of a new name :—that* would have perplexed, rather than comforted. It lay in the hope which the Name afforded, that He who had said to Abram (Gen. xv. 7,) "*I am YAHVEH,* that brought thee out of Ur of the Chaldees, *to give thee this land to inherit it,*" was now about to make good His word of promise.

4. Thus the passage, read along with its context, is not only *not in contradiction* with the passages of Genesis which use the name YAHVEH; but *presupposes* that the name had been known to the patriarchs. Over and over again, it is; ' YAHVEH, *your fathers*' *God,* is about to make Himself known to you.'

How He did so, is evident from the song of Moses: (Exod. xv.): "I will sing unto YAHVEH, for *He has triumphed* gloriously.... Who is like unto Thee, O YAHVEH, among the gods?.... YAHVEH shall reign for ever and ever!" The Redemption out of Egypt was the overt act by which the Theocracy was established. From this time onward "YAHVEH, thy God" became the characteristic mark of true Israelitic faith; as "YAHVEH, He is the God," was the formula by which the Israelites renounced their allegiance to Baal.

5. Consequently, Exod. vi. 2—8, rightly interpreted, proves the baselessness of the supposition, on which the Dismemberers rely for the establishment of their theory; and with the disappearance of that supposition, *cadit quæstio*, their theory collapses.

The whole remaining part of the discussion, therefore, is *ex abundanti*, and a work of charity. The ground on which their argument rests has been cut away from beneath them; they have no fulcrum on which to rest their hypothesis.

We now proceed to shew that, even *supposing* for the time the correctness of their hypothesis, their attempt to dismember Genesis upon that hypothesis is an utter failure.

CHAPTER IV.

Failure of the attempt to employ the Divine Names as a Criterion of diverse Authorship.

THAT the varying use of the Sacred Names, ELOHIM and YAHVEH, was the primary ground on which the Dismemberment Theory took its stand, is evident.

The very names assigned to the supposed writers of the different documents into which the Book of Genesis is to be resolved,—" Elohist," " Second Elohist," " Jehovist," " Second Jehovist," &c.,—implies this.

In many cases there is plainly no other reason than this

for attempting to break up the connexion of passages, as is constantly done by the "critics." Thus, on ch. xx, Dr. Colenso says: (*C. A.*, p. 78):—

"The resemblance between the style of these (later) Elohistic passages and that of the Jehovist is so very great that it becomes at times a matter *of some difficulty to discriminate them.*"

But why *try* to "discriminate" what is so uniform in its texture? Only because the occurrence of the Sacred Names *required* you, on your hypothesis, to make the attempt.

What but this, again, led you to dissever *v.* 18 from the rest of this chapter?

Or what but this suggested the endeavour to rend such a verse as vii. 16 into two parts?

Let us inquire, then, how far the attempt to employ this primary criterion has succeeded.

§ I.

In many cases the decision arrived at by the dismemberers is directly in opposition to what this criterion would warrant.

1. In the last eleven chapters of Genesis, comprising a quarter of the whole book, the sacred name ELOHIM is (with one single exception[1]) exclusively used. Yet eight-ninths of this large section are *not* included by Dr. Colenso in the (supposed) "Elohistic Document," called E, which is taken as the basis of the comparisons set on foot at pp. 18—47.

This single fact is sufficient to vitiate the whole of the attempted process of disintegration.

If the use of the sacred names be taken as the Criterion, ch. xli—xlviii must be assigned to E, quite as much as ch. i or xvii.

So too must ch. xxxiii, of which Dr. Colenso writes; (*C. A.*, p. 79):—

[1] See above p. 17.

"In xxxiii,—a *Jehovistic* chapter, as Hupfeld allows,—'*Elohim*' is used *exclusively*, four times."

3. The testimony of ch. xx, xxi, is similar. Dr. Colenso says, at p. 58:—

"A glance at xx. 1—17 will shew that in this Section *the name 'Elohim' is used exclusively*, (six times,) viz. in *v*. 3, 6, 11, 13, 17; and the same phenomenon occurs again in xxi. 6—22, *where we have 'Elohim' nine times, v.* 6, 12, 17, 19, 20, 22, *and no 'Jehovah.'*"

Yet these two sections, also, are placed in the list of "*non-Elohistic*" passages, (denoted collectively by the term X; p. 18, ff.) Indeed Dr. Colenso is never tired of asserting that this "*Second Elohist*," far from living "*at a very different age*," (see above p. 1) from the 'Jehovist,' *was* "*really one and the same person*," (p. 182). He even enunciates this view in algebraic form thus; $J^1 = E_2$. [u]

And he is, so far, right. There certainly is no reason for doubting the identity of the writer of these chapters with the writer of the passages which he assigns to J.

But then this is a confession that the presumed criterion is *no criterion at all*.

3. Again in ch. xxii. 1—12 the name *Elohim* occurs *five* times, and YAHVEH only once; "which fact," says Hupfeld, (quoted in *C. A.*, p. 93) "*perplexes criticism;*" i.e. the *à priori* criticism, the *uncriticism*, which is (by its own confession) chiefly intent on proving "two main conclusions, ... the *non-Mosaic* authorship of Genesis and the *unhistorical* character of a great portion of its contents." (p. 305.)

There is nothing in the above fact to "perplex" any

---

[u] Cp. p. 66. "This, in short, is the conviction which has been more and more pressed upon me as I have proceeded with this inquiry, *viz.* that *all the difficulties of the case*—the *perplexing phenomena* which have led to *so much difference of opinion* between Hupfeld and Böhmer as to the portions which should be assigned to E_2 and J respectively—may all be explained on the supposition that these 1134 verses [being three-fourths of the whole book] *really belong to one and the same author.*"

honest man, who wishes to conform his opinion to facts, and not make facts bend to a predetermined opinion.

4. Similarly ch. xxxi is assigned to the 'Jehovist,'

"*notwithstanding the fact* that the name 'Elohim' is used as a personal name in it *seven* times, *v.* 7, 9, 16, 24, 42, 50." (*C. A.*, p. 165.)

5. At p. 190, in a concise account of the results of his "Analysis," we find the following:—

"J^1 (E. 22, J. 0); J^2 (E. 67, J. 7);"

that is to say; the "First Set of *Jehoristic* Insertions" contains ELOHIM *twenty-two* times, and the other sacred name *not once;* and the "Second Set of *Jehoristic* Insertions" contains ELOHIM *sixty-seven times* and YAHVEH only *seven*.

One might well ask, on reading such statements;—Is Dr. Colenso's book, after all, not meant to refute the "Critics" in the way of *reductio ad absurdum?* Is he not (as mathematicians are wont to do) adopting a false premiss for the time, in order that by arguing upon it he may arrive at results which will compel the abandonment of the premiss?

§ II.

Impossibility of effecting the desired severance by this Criterion.

This is implied in the formula already quoted, $J^1 = E_2$. For while the *notation* requires us to suppose that two diverse documents have been determined by the criterion of the Sacred Names, the *equation* denies that they *are* diverse.

But we need not infer it by implication; there is abundance of direct evidence to the same effect.

1. At p. 59, Dr. Colenso writes:—

"While the difference in style (if any) between these two writers [J and E_2] is certainly so slight as to afford a very poor criterion for separating their different compositions, this difficulty is increased by the fact that the Jehovist *not unfrequently uses the name 'Elohim,' and sometimes even exclusively.*"

It is understating the case to say merely that "the difficulty is *increased;*"—it is really *insuperable.*

There is absolutely *no* difference of style between the parts of the book, which are assigned to E_2 and J. The truth is, that this fiction of a "Second Elohist" was only adopted to evade the inconvenient facts presented by ch. xx and xxi. E_2 was a bi-frontal being, who might be placed, when necessary, under the general description of "Jehovistic," and yet might be turned round occasionally when the "critics" were hard pressed, and viewed as "Elohistic."

And even this fiction can only be maintained by arbitrarily cutting out certain portions of these chapters: *e.g.* the last verse of ch. xx, (which contains the name YAHVEH). So that the case stands thus:—

Ch. xx contains the name 'YAHVEH,' which you say is *never* used by the "Second Elohist." (*C. A.*, p. 142.) Consequently; either your statement is untrue, if we take the chapter as it is; or, if you wrench v. 18 out of the chapter, you are giving us a mere nugatory statement, when you say that the name 'Yahveh' "never occurs in E_2." How *can* it occur, if, whenever it *does* occur, you *cut it out?*

Either E_2 is "Elohistic," and then you have no right to include it, as you have done, under your X ("non-Elohistic"); or it is "Jehovistic," and then the sacred names clearly can furnish no such criterion as you pretend they do.

2. At *C. A.*, p. 144, he writes:—

"There is, as Hupfeld observes, p. 43, no visible trace of any interruption in the flow of the narrative, or of any connecting link interpolated between the account in xxx. 1, &c., and the preceding context. AND YET *the latter contains only 'Jehovah,'* xxix. 31—33, 35, *which name recurs again in* xxx. 24[b], 27, 30; *while in the interval 'Elohim' is used repeatedly, nine times."*

In other words the narrative, which *ought*, on the application of this criterion, to drop easily asunder, remains inseparably one. There is not so much (it is admitted) as "a trace of a *seam.*" (*C. A.*, p. 153.)

3. He makes xxxv. 1—7 to be "Jehovistic;"—yet the name ELOHIM occurs in it *five times*, and the other sacred name *not once*.

4. In the short passage xxviii. 12—22 the name ELOHIM occurs seven times, and YAHVEH four times; yet the narrative will not bear to be broken up.

What is to be done? Dr. Colenso assigns the whole of it to J.

Yet *within the space of these eleven verses the name ELOHIM occurs as many times as the name YAHVEH occurs in the whole of the First and Second Sets of "Jehovistic Insertions," which comprise* 568 *verses, and contain the name ELOHIM* 89 *times.* That is, briefly;—a ratio of 7 : 89 has strength enough to decide the dominant character of 568 verses, (when the "critics" WILL it;) but a ratio of 7 : 4 has no power to stamp the character of eleven verses, (when the "critics" do *not* WILL it.)

5. At p. 65 we have the following very explicit statement. Any of the opponents of the Disintegrators might have hesitated to write so vigorously for fear of being thought guilty of caricature.

"In fact, even on Hupfeld's showing, something like the above conclusion must follow. He admits that these last eleven chapters of Genesis are made up almost entirely of matter due to E_2 and J, though *he does not attempt to* separate the parts due to these authors. But, *if he had* effected this separation, *it must have appeared that J had not used here* '*Jehovah*' *at all*, except *once* in XLIX. 18, but, on the contrary, *had used exclusively* '*Elohim*;'—UNLESS, indeed, the separation *could have been* effected by him in such a way as to leave to J only portions in which no name of the Deity occurs at all. And this I believe to be IMPOSSIBLE."

That simple narrative—the History of Joseph—baffles all the ingenuity and audacity of a "criticism" which is fettered by nothing short of *impossibility* [x].

---

[x] Dean Milman, speaking of the History of Joseph, says, "The relation in the Book of Genesis is, perhaps, *the most exquisite model* of the manner in

6. We have not, however, yet reached the acme of "critical" self-exposure. At p. 193 Dr. Colenso writes as follows:—

"In J³ we find another step taken in the same direction. The name 'Jehovah' has now, in the latter part of David's reign, become more freely and popularly used; and the writer determines to introduce it at once in his story from the first, *not considering*, apparently, *or not regarding as of any moment, the contradiction which would thus be imported into the narrative*. And, indeed, having already *begun* to employ it in his previous insertions (J²) perhaps he may have thought it best to do this,—*abandoning the Elohistic idea of the origination of the name in the time of Moses*, and representing it as known from the days of the first man downwards. But in order to guard against any mistake, he PERTINACIOUSLY couples the two names together, 'Jehovah—Elohim,' in ii. 4ᵇ—iii. 24 *twenty times*, as if desiring to impress strongly on the reader that the 'Jehovah,' of whom he was about to write, *was the same exactly* as the 'Elohim' of the older writer."

"He *pertinaciously* couples the two names together, *twenty times!*" What stubborn wilfulness,—to throw so serious a difficulty in the way of men who 3,000 years later, in order to prove the book to be "unhistorical," might try to introduce the notion that these names were marks of diverse authorship!

But "*pertinaciously*" intent as this writer was on "guarding against mistake" on this head, yet,—strange to say—he allows a passage to remain uncorrected, which (on Dr. Co-

---

which HISTORY, *without elevating its tone, or departing from its plain and unadorned veracity*, assumes the language and spirit of the most touching poetry." (*Hist. of the Jews*, I. p. 57.)

To the 'critics' this is all imperceptible. "*Non tibi spiro.*" But, if they will not understand its historical beauty, (set aside all thought of its profound theological lessons,) they cannot escape from it. It stands a firm barrier against all their attempts to *de-historicize* "what may be called, by the most modest of its august titles, the oldest and most venerable document of human history.' (Mr. Gladstone's *Address at Edinburgh*.)

lenso's hypothesis) "imports" a glaring "*contradiction*" into the narrative, and that respecting a subject of vital importance. But he did not "consider," or did not "regard as of any moment," the existence of this contradiction,—although the one grand distinguishing peculiarity that *made* him a "Jehovist" was that he had "*abandoned the Elohistic idea of the origination of the Name in the time of Moses.*"

Such are the puerilities, which "criticism" parades before the world, as the means of overthrowing the "historical" character of the book of Genesis. Will it succeed?

No! Dr. Colenso. The men of England may have allowed their theological studies to be too one-sided, and, when surprised by bold assertions, may be staggered for a time; but you have not done justice to the intelligence even of the "working-classes" (p. xliii), if you think they are unable to see through, and to pass sentence on, such writing as the above. It cannot be long before they make up their minds as to *who* the *poco-curante* party is. They cannot long doubt whether the man who has scattered contradictions over his writings, and then borne himself so lightly and heedlessly in the midst of them, be Dr. Colenso himself, or one of those whom even *he* is obliged to speak of as "*good and great men,* . . . leading men of their respective ages.*" (p. 180.)

7. One more proof, and we close the chapter.

The xvii[th] chapter is looked upon as "*the Elohistic model section.*" Yet the name YAHVEH lies firmly imbedded in the very first verse.

"*This phenomenon,*" says Dr. Colenso, "*has perplexed ALL CRITICAL COMMENTATORS.*"

Similar "perplexities" occur in dealing with chapters xxii and xlix; but there the difficulties presented by the occurrence of this name 'YAHVEH' may be evaded (though with great difficulty) by *calling* the chapters "Jehovistic." But if this method were applied to ch. xvii, the whole disintegration-scheme would have to be surrendered at once.

What then is to be done? The only resource is to *get rid of the evidence*, by altering the text. Hupfeld hints at the *possibility* of resorting to what he allows to be "a doubtful assumption;" but Dr. Colenso has no such delicacy. He says unhesitatingly: "*I conclude*, that the original text is here *corrupted.*"

That is, he admits that his view *cannot be held consistently with the* FACTS, *which he is pretending to analyse*. In other words, either he or facts must give way.

Accordingly he proceeds to set in motion all his machinery for crushing facts. (*C. A.*, p. 67.) "The name may have 'slipt in' by an *oversight* on the part of the original writer," "or by an *interpolation* of a later Compiler," "or by a mere *error of transcription :*"—at any rate, it "has been changed *somehow.*" Why? The only reason is,—it is necessary for their purpose to have it so.

The legitimate argument would run thus: "If our scheme for the dismemberment of Genesis were correct, there *ought to be* 'ELOHIM' in ver. 1.—But this is *not* the case; therefore our scheme cannot stand."

In spite of this clear evidence, however, Dr. Colenso continues his course unmoved: and at a later page (*C. A.*, p. 142) does not scruple to make this assertion :—

"The Elohist never uses 'Jehovah' throughout the book of Genesis."

Much more might easily be added [y]; but I am willing to leave any honest mind to supply the verdict on the evidence already given.

Has it not been amply proved that—even granting the "critics" full liberty, for the time, to employ their (groundless) hypothesis,—the book of Genesis *cannot* be severed by

---

[y] We shall have to recur to this subject—the violent methods adopted by the Dismemberers,—at a later period.

employing the two Sacred Names as a criterion of diverse authorship?

The reader will be pleased to bear in mind that in this chapter we have been exhibiting the inefficacy of the "critical" mode of procedure, *even upon their own hypothesis*,—that hypothesis itself having previously been proved to be contradictory to facts, and therefore worthless.

SECTION II.

ON THE ENDEAVOUR TO MAKE OUT A DIVERSITY OF STYLE
WITH A VIEW TO THE DISMEMBERMENT
OF GENESIS.

"The idea that the poem [the Iliad] as we read it grew out of atoms not originally designed for the places which they now occupy, *involves us in new and inextricable difficulties* when we seek to elucidate either the mode of coalescence or the degree of existing unity.

"The advocates of the Wolfian theory appear to feel the difficulties which beset it; for *their language is wavering in respect to their supposed primary atoms*. . . . .

"But if it be granted that the original constituent songs were so composed, though by different poets, as that the more recent were adapted to the earlier, with more or less of dexterity and success, this brings us into totally different conditions of the problem; *it is a virtual surrender of the Wolfian hypothesis*, which however Lachmann both means to defend, and does defend with ability; though his vindication of it has, to my mind, only the effect of EXPOSING ITS INHERENT WEAKNESS, BY CARRYING IT OUT INTO SOMETHING DETAILED AND POSITIVE."

MR. GROTE, *History of Greece*, (ii. 232).

"For my part, I decline to discard any item of the Thrasyllian Canon, upon such evidence as they produce: I think it is a safer and more philosophical proceeding to accept the entire Canon, and to *accommodate my general theory of Plato* (so far as I am able to frame one) *to each and all of its contents*."

MR. GROTE, *Plato*, (i. 206).

CHAPTER I.

The Character of the so-called Argument from "Style."

1. Dr. Colenso is constantly speaking of the different *styles* of the writers, E and J. Nay, it would seem as if he had some philological test by which he can discriminate certain slighter changes of style in the same writer, so that he can divide what was written by J at an early period (J^1 or E_2) from what he wrote at a later period (J^2). He thinks he can decide that the writer has been "*increasing in ease and fluency.*" (p. 65.)

It may not be improper to ask what qualifications a person who undertakes to make such nice distinctions in the style of a Hebrew writer has brought to his task. This will be briefly examined into in the appendix to this chapter. At present I wish only to call attention to what Dr. Colenso *means* by the word "STYLE."

2. We all know what a subtle thing "style" is;—"quod nequeo monstrare et sentio tantum." Sometimes it has peculiarities of grammatical inflexion associated with it; more frequently it arises from the arrangement of words in a clause, the rhythm of its sentences, or the introduction of slight *nuances* in the meaning of words. These, however, do not enter at all into Dr. Colenso's notion of style.

Again, in a composite language like English, the mere vocabulary comes into consideration as an element of style. One style savours more of Latin, another of Saxon, &c. But it is not even alleged that there is anything of *this* kind possible in Hebrew, which is a simple, and not a composite, language.

3. Dr. Colenso's notion of *style* is quite different from aught hitherto mentioned. According to his argument, *the*

recurrence of the same words constitutes identity of style; the *want of such recurrence* implies difference of style;— difference of style in such a sense as compels us to infer diversity of authorship. Each writer is supposed to have at his disposal a limited number of *"formulæ"* (p. 27), within the range of which he must work. He *must* in each chapter employ these "formulæ," and these only. He must be content with one small portion of his mother-tongue, and not dare to venture across the limits of that portion,—on pain of losing his identity. Consequently, (on Dr. Colenso's hypothesis,) if I find words present in one part of a book which are absent from another part, I am warranted in concluding that these two parts were written by different authors.

4. It might seem unnecessary to point out the absurdity of such a view. What would be thought of any man who tried to apply it to the decomposition, *e.g.*, of Herodotus?

When Herodotus is describing Babylon, Egypt, and Scythia, he uses different words from those that occur in the speeches of Artabanus and Mardonius. Of course, it was impossible for him to do otherwise. Who ever dreamt of asserting that this implied any difference of "style," and that we must on this account break up the "Nine Muses" between several authors?

Yet this would be precisely analogous to what the "critics," whom Dr. Colenso follows, have attempted to do with the book of Genesis.

E.g. In the description of the preparation of the Earth for man's inhabitation, and in the narratives of God's covenants with Noah and Abraham, many terms are used which were not likely to occur in the history of Joseph. Conversely, many words (" comfort," " fear," " love," &c.) occur in this history which were *not wanted* in the account of the Six Days' work. Does this justify us in inferring a difference of style between these parts, and a consequent diversity of authorship?

According to Dr. Colenso's argument throughout his

Analysis it *does*. By far the greater part of the words, phrases, and "formulæ," on which his dissection of Genesis rests, are simple and easy words[a], with which any intelligent writer must have been familiar; yet because they are not scattered indiscriminately over the whole book,—because they are not found, where they were not wanted,—we are to demand a diversity of authors, one for the places where they do occur, and another for those where they do not.

He never could have attributed one particle of weight to such a method of reasoning, unless he had previously made up his mind that the dismemberment must be attempted *somehow*. The argument is devoid of any logical basis whatever.

We might fairly abstain, then, from noticing this argument from "style" any further. But as our object is to satisfy and convince, as well as to refute, we purpose, (as in the former section, so here,) to follow Dr. Colenso's actual argument into its details, and shew *ex abundanti* that (even on the "critic's" own standing-ground) this verbal "analysis" is utterly ineffectual to the purpose for which it was employed.

APPENDIX *TO* CHAP. I.

On Dr. Colenso's qualifications for conducting an inquiry into Hebrew "style"[b].

A FEW instances will suffice to enable the reader to form an opinion about Dr. Colenso's competency for executing so delicate a task.

---

[a] E.g. "To send," "tell," "know," "place," "serve," "find," "leave," "slay," "grow," "run," "weep," "love," "hate," "fear," "word," "dream," "lad," "tent," "behind," "beside," "a little water," "a little food," "in that day," "in that night," "perhaps."—Dr. Colenso admits in one place that such expressions "*might* have been used by the Elohist, and *probably would be found used by him*, whenever the occasion required it." (p. 35.) It follows, therefore, that so far as what he calls "style" is concerned, there is no reason why E and J might not be one and the same person; which is just to undo all that his 300 pages of "Analysis" are toiling so painfully to effect.

[b] I would gladly have spared both myself and Dr. Colenso the pain of such

1. What shall we say of his mis-spelling at least *eight* times[c] (and I think invariably) so common a word as the pronoun of the first person sing., אָנֹכִי? He writes it אָנֹכִי; and in *four* out of the eight places has enforced his wrong spelling by printing it in Italic thus; "*ănochi.*"

This is much as if a person undertaking to dismember the Gospel of St. Matthew were to tabulate the pronoun of the first person plural thus, [ἐμεις, "*hēmeis.*"]

2. Hebrew phrases, which are of common occurrence, are rendered by Dr. Colenso with a startling awkwardness of English phrase, which certainly does not suggest the idea of familiarity with the language. E.g.

(a) He several times renders עֶצֶם, ("the same,") by, "the bone of." See p. 7, 19, 200, and *C. A.*, p. 25, 70. Similarly in "analyzing" a French work, one might produce a large number of striking idiosyncrasies of language on almost any page by translating in this way; "*beaucoup* d'esprit,—*fine-blow* of spirit;" "je ne sais *pas*—I not know *a step.*"

(b) He renders שְׂפַת הַיָּם, "the *lip* of the sea:" (p. 32, 268, *C. A.*, p. 96). So a beginner in Latin might render "sinus Ionicus" by "the Ionian *bosom.*"

(c) He translates לְפִי, "*at the mouth of*," (p. 229, cp. *C. A.*, p. 224). As if one were to render "au pied de la lettre—*at the foot of* the letter."

3. At p. 29 he writes the fem. of יֶלֶד, as if it were the same as the fem. third pers. pret. of the verb, thus: "יָלְדָה, *yălĕdah:*" just as great a blunder as if a boy having to give the fem. of φίλος were to write it thus; "φιλει, *philei.*"

4. At p. 229 he renders העד בנו, (E.V. rightly "protested *unto* us") by "protested *among* us;" shewing that he was not acquainted with so simple a construction as העד ב. At

an exposure. But it would be no kindness to *him* to omit it; and a regard to the truth, which he has so vehemently persecuted, and to the prophets and saints of God, whom he has disparaged and calumniated, demands its insertion. I shall confine myself to a simple exposition of *facts*. Let others judge of the inferences that must issue out of them.

[c] See p. 19, 24, (twice,) 25, 27 (twice); and *C. A.*, 20, 98.

this rate we ought to make Solomon (1 Kings ii. 42) address Shimei thus : " Did I not protest *among* thee ?"

5. These are all cases that belong to the rudimentary knowledge of Hebrew. Of course, one who could make mistakes like the above cannot possibly have entered into the nicer distinctions of grammar. Indeed, I do not remember to have observed in any part of the volume a single trace of his being even conscious of the existence of the more special rules of Hebrew syntax.

Take the following remark as a specimen in this department, (*C. A.*, p. 217) :—

" xli. 12, ' and there was there with us a Hebrew boy.'

" .... Perhaps the Hebrew should be pointed—not וְשָׁם, ' and there,' but—וַיָּשֶׂם ' and he placed,' *comp.* xxx. 41."

This proves that he does not understand anything of the laws of the Tenses. Every Hebrew scholar knows that וַיָּשֶׂם *could not possibly* stand here;—we should want of necessity וַיָּשֶׂם.

He was evidently misled by xxx. 41, where וַיָּשֶׂם occurs, but *in an entirely different construction, viz.* as a frequentative; which is proved (not that there is *need* of proof) by the לֹא־יָשִׂים of *v.* 42 [d].

6. The above cases all refer to simple *grammar;*—a knowledge of which is commonly thought essential to a critic. Let me add one out of many specimens of Dr. Colenso's qualifications for the work of exegesis.

There is a narrative in ch. xxi. full of tenderness, but containing *one word,* (in *v.* 15,) which has been misunder-

---

[d] Not to let this rest only on my assertion, let me refer to Ewald, *Ausf. Lehrb. der Hebr. S.* ; § 342, *b.*; where this very passage (xxx. 41) is referred to as an example of the " perfectum consecutivum " used " bei Schilderung dauernder oder *oft wiederholter Thaten*," .... " indem mitten an die Erzählung einmal geschehener Dinge auch etwas als mehr weilend oder *sich wiederholend* angeknüpft werden kann, 1 Sam. 1, 3. 7, 15 f. 16, 23. 17, 20. Gen. 30. 41 f. 38, 9. 2 Kön. 6, 10. 21, 6."

stood. Still,—in spite of this,—the touching beauty of the narrative is most evident.

Dean Milman—himself both poet and historian—observes: "*History or poetry scarcely presents us with any passage which surpasses in simple pathos the description of Hagar, not daring to look upon her child, while he is perishing with thirst.*"

See, now, how Dr. Colenso treats this narrative. (*C. A.*, p. 87.) "The expressions in *v.* 14, 15, 20 are not inconsistent with the idea of Ishmael's being a great boy of fourteen, even supposing that his mother carried him on her back; SINCE Umkungo, son of Umpande, King of the Zulus, was just such a lad as this, *and very fat*, when he fled from his brother's fury not long ago; and he was then carried by his mother, and *might have been* 'cast under a tree' by her, if dying from thirst."

Such is the delicate handling the passage receives from him.

Now, as a matter of fact, it is quite plain that in the Hebrew nothing occurs, which in any way countenances the notion that Ishmael was placed on Hagar's back. And, secondly, if Dr. Çolenso had given a few minutes to thinking over the LXX. rendering of וַתַּשְׁלֵךְ, καὶ ἔρριψεν, he might have seen a new proof of the admirable tenderness of the whole description. For this is the very word used in St. Matt. xv. 30 of laying the sick "at the feet of Jesus:" (ἔρριψαν αὐτούς). It represented the affectionate service which friendship rendered to the "lame, the blind, the deaf, the maimed, *and many others.*" The Egyptian mother had borne the day's exposure to the sun in the desert; the boy by her side fainted; and a mother's loving hands "*laid him*" in all his helplessness [e] "*prostrate on the ground.*"

---

[e] Cp. the use of the Hophal in Ps. xxii. 11; "Upon Thee have I been cast from the womb."

CHAPTER II.
The Worth of the Phraseological Test.

§ I.
It is admitted, in general, by the "critics" themselves to be ineffectual.

WE have already had occasion to notice this; (above p. 22, 25). But we again venture to subpœna Dr. Colenso to give evidence.

He says:—

"Every favourite formula used by the Second Elohist is used also by the Jehovist." (p. 67.)

"The style of the two writers [E_2 and J] *is so very similar*[f], except in the use of the Divine Name, that *it is impossible* to distinguish them by considerations of style alone." (p. 59.)

"The phraseology employed *throughout* the history of Joseph is *quite Jehovistic:* and, though, it is true, two distinct stories may be traced in it[g], yet in the *style* of these stories there is no essential difference that we have been able to detect; *in both, the same phrases are employed*, as they are by the Jehovist in passages which are undoubtedly his: in both, *the name 'Elohim' is used exclusively*, when the Divine Name is used at all." (p. 65.)

We could not desire a more full and unsuspected testimony to the fact that phraseology cannot effect a severance of the (supposed) "Elohistic" and "Jehovistic" elements, sought for by the Disintegrators.

We shall, therefore, proceed at once to confirm this general testimony by particular instances.

§ II.
Instances of the worthlessness of the argument.

1. Let us take as a first example an application of it, on which Dr. Colenso appears to have laid much stress. In the

---

[f] As regards this euphemistic way of writing, see above, p. 25. There is *no* difference whatever in the style of the two portions so designated. K.

[g] The "*traces*" are simply insertions of the "critics;"—which have to be maintained by such emendations as the one we lately examined at p. 37;—and by violent distortions of fact, such as will be noticed hereafter. K.

preface to his translation of Kuenen's "Pentateuch critically examined,"—which was published in this present year (1865,)—he goes somewhat out of his way to give prominence to the following observation :—

"In addition to the *linguistic* evidence produced by Professor Kuenen in (46), and by myself in Part III. chap. 1, to show that the Deuteronomist was a very different person from the writer (or writers) of the main portion of the other four Books of the Pentateuch, it may be noted that of the two Hebrew words for 'heart,' לב *lev* and לֵבָב *levav*,—

"The former occurs *sixty-two* times in Genesis, Exodus, Leviticus, Numbers, and only *four* times in Deuteronomy. . . .

"The latter occurs only *eight* times in Genesis, Exodus, Leviticus, Numbers, ... and *forty-six* times in Deuteronomy."

Here, then, is a fair case for testing the value of the argument. One would think that if it could be sustained anywhere, it must be here. If *this* induction break down, the method itself surely must be intrinsically vicious.

We need not enter into any inquiry as to the true explanation of the above facts. Dr. Colenso himself shall be our voucher for one other *fact*, which will make the seemingly terrible induction prove perfectly harmless. For on Gen. xxxi. 26 he writes thus: (*C. A.*, p. 162) :—

"N.B. In *v*. 26 we have לֵבָב 'heart,' and in *v*. 20 לֵב,—*manifestly by the same writer.*"

Whatever then be the explanation of the use of the two forms, so much at least is certain, that it does not imply diversity of authorship. Consequently, we have here a MANIFEST proof, that the method pursued by the "critics" is valueless. The high-towering theory, which was built up with so much toil, and which looked at first so imposing, is laid low in a moment.

2. Another simple instance of the failure of the "critical" method is supplied by the word קְלָלָה: (*C. A.*, p. 129). It occurs *ten times* in the book of Deuteronomy, and only *once* in the four preceding books, viz. in Gen. xxvii. 13. This

CHAP. II.] *A seemingly strong induction proved valueless.* 41

verse, therefore, *ought* (on the "critical" theory) to be from the "Deuteronomist." But it cannot possibly be taken out from the body of the chapter; which has been given to J.

Here then we have a case of induction a thousand-fold stronger than is to be found in nineteen-twentieths of this "Critical Analysis," which yet turns out to be plainly of no value whatever. An infinite number of such cases must, therefore, be absolutely worthless: for $0 + 0 + 0$ ad inf. $= 0$.

3. At p. 28, where he is assigning vii. 21, 22 to the "Elohist," he says:—

"N.B. The word for 'dry land' in vii. 22 is הָרָבָה, which differs from that in i. 9, 10, יַבָּשָׁה [h]; but neither of these occurs again in Genesis; and the verb הָרַב, 'be dried up,' occurs in viii. 13 (E) 13[b] (J), and יָבֵשׁ in viii. 14 (E), viii. 7 (J)."

A pretty complication for the phraseologist to encounter! (1) The *same* writer is to be allowed to use two *different* "formulæ" without resigning his identity:—and then (2) each of these "formulæ" is employed by *both* E and J. It would be difficult to devise a neater way of disproving both parts of the phraseological canon.

4. An exquisite illustration of the value of the "phraseological" argument is given in *C. A.*, pp. 40, 42; where *the very same phrases* are adduced on separate pages as indicating the hand of *different* writers.

At p. 40, Dr. Colenso, wishing to assign x. 8—12 to the (imaginary) "Deuteronomist," writes:—

"(v.) *v.* 8. הֵחֵל, 'begin,' D. ii. 24, 25, 31, 31, iii. 24, xvi. 9, 9. Jo. iii. 7. (D).

"(viii.) *v.* 9, עַל־כֵּן 'therefore.' D. x. 9."

Now on reading this, one is naturally disposed to ask whether such common words as "therefore," and "begin," are sufficiently *characteristic* to justify our resting so weighty an argument upon them. Still, *there is the evidence :—* clear, definite, and reduced to almost mathematical precision.

[h] Dr. Colenso's way of spelling יַבָּשָׁה.

There, too, are *the actual Hebrew words* quoted. How can we resist the inference?—Rather, how can we hope to *refute* persons, who are satisfied to think that *any* grounds for inference have been supplied?

The case seems all but hopeless, either way.

But no;—turn over one leaf, and your fears will be dispelled. It is but a set of "dissolving views" that is passing in front of us. No Archimage ever raised an enchanted castle more readily than the " critics;" but none can knock them down (when required) more readily.

At p. 42 wishing to make out[1] that xi. 1—9 belongs to the "Jehovist," Dr. Colenso confronts us with the following evidence.

"*xi. v. 6. הֵחֵל *hekhel,* 'begin' (5. xxix.)

"*xiii. v. 9. עַל־כֵּן, 'therefore.' (3. xvii.)"

The asterisc (*) denotes that the words are used only by *one* writer throughout the book of Genesis,'—in this case the "*Jehovist;*"—while the annotations "(5. xxix.)" and "(3. xvii.)" refer to the following statements: (*C.A.*, pp. 11 and 7.)

"(xxix.) *v.* 26. הֵחֵל 'begin,' iv. 26. vi. 1. ix. 20. x. 8. xi. 6. xli. 54. xliv. 12, also D. (x. 8).

"(xvii.) *v.* 24. עַל־כֵּן, 'therefore,' ii. 24. xi. 9. xvi. 14, xviii. 5. xix. 8, 22. xx. 6ᵇ. xxi. 31. xxxii. 32 (33). xxxiii. 10, 17. xxxviii. 26. xlii. 21. xlvii. 22: also D. (x. 9.)"

Thus the same words in one place show a "Deuterono-

---

[1] I do not use this expression at random. The "wish" is apparent on the very surface of his book. Dr. Colenso himself not unfrequently speaks as if unconscious that there is anything wrong in making "the wish father to the thought" in such an inquiry. For instance, he says of one of his chief guides, (*C. A.*, p. 64): "Boehmer, *wishing to secure for E_2* an independent account of the birth of Ishmael, *assigns to him v.* 2 and *v.* 15ᵃ."

Compare, also, the following. "Boehmer gives the above to the Compiler—*chiefly because* by assigning it to the Jehovist, he would *seriously compromise his other conclusions.*" (*C. A.*, p. 243.) And: "The fact is that his 'Compiler' is frequently *very useful in taking charge of passages* which give strong indications of one of the *other two* sources." (Ib., p. 249.)

mistic" face; in another they are exclusively "*Jehovistic*;" in another they are bifrontal, indicating *both* J and D.

Surely something more than a verdict of simple "*nihil probatur*" is called for by such futilities as these. *A great deal* is proved by them, as to the value of the *method* of reasoning employed by the "critics."

CHAPTER III.

On the Way in which the Test is applied.

1. In Dr. Colenso's hands the application of the test admits of every degree of stringency or laxity. (A) In some cases, the most ordinary words or phrases are diligently collected, and treated with high respect as proofs of *identity* of authorship; whilst the slightest possible variations are insisted upon as marks of *diversity*. (B) In other cases the evidence of really important words and phrases is set aside with a stroke of the pen.

2. Instances of (A) need scarcely be produced. They meet one on every page. Let the following serve as specimens:—

At pp. 74—76, e.g., we find "therefore," "wash your feet," "your servant," "do evil," "thy soul," "except," "that night," used as marks of the "Jehovistic" character of ch. xix.

But at p. 38 he remarks:—

"i. v. 1. 'And these are the generations of the *sons of Noah*.' No formula like this occurs among the E formulæ in (2. iii); and E *would hardly have written this*, INASMUCH AS *he writes* in xi. 10, 'these are the generations of *Shem*.'"

The authors he has pictured to himself must have been indeed cast-iron puppets,—of less ability than the "calculating machine,"—if their power of varying their "formulæ" did not extend far enough to allow of their introducing such a change as this.

3. As instances of (B) take the following:—

(*a*) The occurrence of some words and phrases, which the "critics" have considered to be 'Elohistic,' has led Knobel and Delitzsch to assign ch. xxxiv. to E. Dr. Colenso admits that "the coincidences [in ver. 23] are certainly remarkable." The word קָרָה, in particular, a rare word, occurs only in two other places in the Pentateuch, and both these are in portions assigned to E. But then, says Dr. Colenso with unwonted keenness of vision, "the fact that E has it *twice*, cannot be sufficient to *assure* it to him as *exclusively* Elohistic."

So too the word נָשִׂיא in *v*. 2 is used in three other places of Genesis by E, by J not once.

But Dr. Colenso is inexorable. "The whole chapter belongs to J."

(*b*) The verb נסע, which occurs in Genesis only in the (supposed) "Jehovistic" passages, is found also in the section, xxxv. 16—20: and Hupfeld actually assigns this section to J. Dr. Colenso, however, will have it belong to E, and remarks that the word נסע

"does not, indeed, occur in any other passage of E in Genesis; —*but merely*, it would seem, *because this writer has not required to use it*. . . . It is, in fact, *the word that he would naturally use*, if he wanted to express the breaking up of an encampment."

If this (very obvious) reflexion were but fairly carried out, it would destroy the theory on which the pretended "Analysis" rests.

APPENDIX *TO* CHAP. III.
On Ps. lxviii. 1.

1. Dr. Colenso has felt himself hard pressed with the fact that in Ps. lxviii. 1 we have a quotation from Numb. x. 35;

—but with this difference, that the Psalmist has changed the YAHVEH of the earlier formula into ELOHIM. This, of course, is contradictory to his theory of the late introduction of the former name. He therefore calls into operation those arbitrary processes, which recur with sickening sameness throughout his pseudo-criticism.

The passage in Numbers, he says, is an *interpolation*. It was written by the *Deuteronomist*; (as, no doubt, it *was* really; but he means by the term an unknown writer conjectured to have lived about the time of Josiah.) It was copied from the Psalm; the interpolator changing the ELOHIM of the Psalm into YAHVEH.

2. Let us see how far this view is borne out, then, by the phraseological "analysis" of Ps. lxviii. 1.

קוּם is stated by Dr. Colenso to occur *twenty* times in the "Jehovistic" parts of Genesis, (p. 26), and is marked by him with an asterisc as *exclusively* belonging to J.

פוּץ occurs in Gen. ix. 19. x. 18. xi. 4, 8, 9. xlix. 7, (all assigned to J: see *C. A.*, p. 36).

איב in Gen. xxii. 17. xlix. 8; (*both* "non-Elohistic;" the former Deuteronomistic).

נוּס. xiv. 10 (twice). xix. 20. xxxix. 12, 13, 14, 15. (All "Jehovistic.")

שׂנא : seven times in J :—and asteriscized; (*C. A.*, p. 132).

All this "Jehovistic" phraseology is congregated in a single verse. Surely, then, (*ex hypothesi*) this verse *must* be essentially "Jehovistic." It follows that that form of the verse in which the name YAHVEH occurs, namely Numb. x. 34, must be the primitive one. Consequently we have here an "Elohistic" writer (as Dr. Colenso considers the composer of Ps. lxviii. to have been) borrowing from a "Jehovistic" passage :—a fact at variance with the fundamental assumption of the Disintegrators.

Thus then—on his own chosen ground—he is reduced to the following alternative :—

Either the above words are n٠t "Jehovistic," and then the

"Analysis" of Genesis is proved to be a spider's web:—or if they *are* "Jehovistic," then Numb. x. 34 is the original, and the theory of the late origin of the Sacred Name YAHVEH crumbles to dust.

CHAPTER IV.

The kind of Manipulation by which the "Analyst" has got at his Results.

1. THE object of the so-called "Critical Analysis" is to separate the book of Genesis into certain (supposed) component documents. To effect this the Critic ought to have some well-defined principle in his possession. What then is this principle?

The occurrence of the Divine names? No. We saw that this *could* not furnish the criterion required.

Difference of style? We have seen that no such difference can be established.

Is it, then, by means of the occurrence of certain words which are respectively "Elohistic" and "Jehovistic?" Is this the test by which the character of the several portions of Genesis is to be determined? So it would seem.

But then the question arises, how do we *know* what words *are* "Elohistic" or "Jehovistic?" Are we to decide this by looking to see where the words occur,—whether in document E, or in document J? This is the method generally pursued by Dr. Colenso and his guides.

So, then, you tell us to determine the documents by means of the words, and the words by means of the documents;— a plainly vicious circle of investigation. Yet this is the staple of your "Analysis."

2. This vicious circle can only be escaped from by taking lower ground, and acknowledging that the process is not ruled by any definite principle, but is merely a *tentative* one.

A guess is made, that certain words *may possibly* be found characteristic of certain portions, which *may possibly* turn out also to correspond to the parts in which the two sacred Names severally predominate.

This being the case, it is evident that the Investigator is bound to go to work *very modestly;* resolving to obey the guidance of facts, and never to over-ride any strong presumptions which may oppose his advance. This is plainly the duty of an inquirer who sets out with nothing beyond the merest *possibility* on his side.

3. Dr. Colenso's method of proceeding, however, is just the reverse of this. E.g. Having laid it down, from a rough survey of a certain portion of Genesis, that certain words shall be considered "Elohistic," he insists thenceforward on maintaining his assumption at all hazards. If a passage containing any of these words be produced from a chapter which is naturally assigned to J, instead of retreating and giving up his assumption, he despotically wrenches the passage from its context, and gives it—poor maimed fragment as it is—to E.

Having thus "secured" this and that portion of his document *by means of* his arbitrarily assumed test-words, he at last (after completing his circuit) turns round and asks us to admire the fact that these words occur *only* in that particular document; and invites us to accept this surprising circumstance as a proof that the document must have a real existence.

4. It is not necessary that I should prove what I have asserted by many examples. The "vicious circle" recurs with wearisome iteration throughout the "Analysis." Two or three of the more important instances, well sifted, will enable the reader to arrive at a fair judgment on the whole question.

(*a*) Ch. xxxi., which contains fifty-five verses, is pronounced by the "Analyst" to be "Jehovistic,"—*with the solitary exception* of *v.* 18. The general presumption against thus detaching a single verse is evidently very great; and this is increased enormously when we find (1) that the loss of the verse would make the narrative limp: and (2) that the fragment has no connexion with the "Elohistic" document to which it is proposed to transfer it. The new "Elohistic" narrative reads — not merely "abruptly," (as Dr. Colenso far too gently remarks, *C. A.*, p. 164,) but—quite absurdly.

"And she conceived and bare a son, and she said, 'Elohim hath gathered my reproach.' And she called his name Joseph. And he led away all his cattle and all his goods, which he had gotten."

But why, it may be asked, should any one *wish* to disturb the verse?

So far as appears, the reason is, because it had been *conjectured*—or desired—that the words, "he led off all his cattle and all his goods (רְכֻשׁוֹ) which he had gotten" *might* be 'secured' as "Elohistic."

The "*Analyst*," indeed, took the liberty of attaching an asterisc (*) to the phrase as early as *C. A.*, p. 46 (on xii. 5); but that could only, at *that stage of the inquiry*, indicate a guess or a wish on his part. The fact cannot have been *inductively* ascertained; for we see that the phrase occurs here in a "Jehovistic" chapter.

But how about even that former passage (xii. 5)? Does that so clearly belong to E? Not at all. The case is nearly the same with it as with xxxi. 18. *First:* Ch. xii is allowed to be as a whole "Jehovistic;" and when 4^b, 5, have been rent from it and transferred to the (imagined) E document, the fragment "stands" (by Dr. Colenso's own confession, *C. A.*, p. 161) "just as abruptly," as xxxi. 18 does.

Here, then, again we have to bow before some mysterious and unexplained *necessity*, perceived by our guide the "Analyst," though hidden from us. Perhaps we may get more light as we advance; for the word רְכוּשׁ occurs again in xiii. 6, and again (remarkably enough) has the effect of detaching a single verse from a "Jehovistic" chapter. But the *reason*

CHAP. IV.] *'Critical' Intuition mightier than Induction.* 49

of this is not yet apparent. For the present we must be satisfied with the Analyst's "stet pro ratione *voluntas.*" *He*, no doubt, has certain valid *subjective* reasons. We must *trust* him,—as Hupfeld warned us above [k].

But the mystery grows still darker when we pass to ch. xiv. In this chapter we find the following clauses :—

v. 11. "and they took all the goods (רכש) of Sodom . . ."

v. 12. "and they took Lot and his goods (רכש) . . ."

v. 16. "and he brought back all the goods (רכש); and also Lot, his brother, and his goods (רכש) he brought back."

v. 21. "Give me the persons (נפש) and the goods (רכש) take for thyself."

Here, we should have thought, the power of this influential word could easily have made itself felt. But the "Analyst" thinks otherwise. He assigns the chapter to the "*Second Jehorist*,"—"*whose hand cannot be traced* in any other part of the Pentateuch ;" (*C. A.*, p. 53).

This is hard measure ; after having rent verses away from J, because of this phrase, to allow it now to stand freely in J$_2$.—But, after all, these are only "*slight* points of contact," (so we are told in *C. A.*, p. 54,) between E and J$_2$, which *prove nothing :*—whence, perhaps, we may account for the otherwise surprising circumstance that the "Analyst" has made bold to insert the phrase *with an asterisc* in the "Elohistic" list : (p. 20. xx.)

But *why* are the *four* phrases so feeble here, when *one* of them has been on three several occasions found so mighty ?

It is clear that we must be patient. *Intuition* is not gained at once. Have not Ilgen and Knobel and Tuch, Hupfeld and Böhmer and Stähelin, and others, got at last through these and countless other similar, or greater, difficulties ? We must not insist too much on the Baconian views of Induction.—*These*, by making *facts* take precedence of *wishes*, would clearly lead us to treat רכש as a thoroughly "Jehovistic" term ; [supposing such a distinction to exist

[k] See Note at p. 3.

E

at all]. Let us, then, discard those views and proceed with our "Analysis."

The word רכש occurs again in ch. xv. But here the "Analyst" does not even notice the word. It reposes undisturbed in the midst of a chapter which he pronounces, (oh marvellous power of intuition!) to belong wholly to the "*Deuteronomist.*"

The only other places in Genesis where the word occurs are xxxvi. 7, and xlvi. 6; but these do not explain why so much decision should have been exhibited in handling the previous passages.

On looking back, however, on the whole range of passages, *one* explanation offers itself. May it not be that the object was to 'secure' xii. 5 to E at all risks;—because without this the "Elohistic" document would have no way of commencing its history of Abraham?—Here then, at last, is the hidden spring from which the wonder-working "intuition" welled forth. Genesis MUST *be broken up into parts:*—this is to be our guiding principle. This shall inspire us with indomitable perseverance in the midst of the most serious difficulties, no matter what resistance we may meet with from facts.

(*b*) Again: ch. xxiv contains 67 verses. The whole of it is ascribed to J, with the exception of *vv.* 59, 60. I will venture to say, that no one having the slightest power of appreciating that beautiful narrative,—viewed, if you will, from a mere literary standpoint,—would consent to such a mutilation, unless the very strongest evidence of its necessity could be produced. What then is the evidence? The only "phrase" marked by Dr. Colenso with an asterisc is this: "'Thy seed shall occupy the gate of his enemies;"—a saying which had occurred in xxii. 17, and occurs *nowhere else in the Bible.* Yet Dr. Colenso holds that it is a "Deuteronomistic" phrase.

How can this be? Is there anything in ch. xxii to drive us to this conclusion?

CHAP. IV.] *How* אחת *is proved to be "Elohistic."* 51

Hupfeld says of ch. xxii, that it is "a complete, well-adjusted whole," and that "the whole narrative in spirit and form seems to bear the stamp of the *Jehovist*." (*C. A.*, p. 93.)

Why, then, should this well-adjusted whole be broken up?

Because criticism has a quarrel with the chapter[1],—in which Abraham's faith attains its culminating point,—and must endeavour in some way or other to lacerate it.

(*c*) At p. 21 Dr. Colenso marks אֶחָדּ with an asterisc, as exclusively "Elohistic." Yet it occurs in xxxvi. 43, which Hupfeld denies to be part of E. It occurs, too, in xlvii. 11, no part of which is given by Hupfeld to E: and Dr. Colenso, who gives it to E, can only attain his point by cutting up the single verse in this most remarkable manner,

11^{ab} (E), 11^c (J), 11^d (E), 11^e (J).

The word occurs again in l. 13; which verse cannot be severed from the context; and the chapter as a whole is given by Dr. Colenso to J.

It must, therefore, be *intuition*, (for it is certainly not *induction*,) that settles the question.

(*d*) At p. 29 he places the word כַּוִּּר, with an asterisc, on the non-Elohistic list.

Yet the very first passage he quotes in proof of its belonging to J,—*viz.* viii. 13^b—lies in the midst of a Section (13—19) which he allots to E: and when we look for the reason of his thus tearing 13^b out of its natural abode, we find this very word כַּוִּּר to be the main evidence adduced.— The old vicious circle.

(*e*) One more instance, and we have done.

In *C. A.*, p. 74—77, he makes the whole of ch. xix to be "Jehovistic" with the exception of *v.* 29. Why hold this to be an exception?

Because *v.* 29, he thinks, is "a strange and tame conclusion" to the narrative.—The exact contrary is true.—It is a most striking and pregnant piece of information; which

[1] Cp. above, p. 23.

binds the events just narrated into close connexion with Abraham's intercession in ch. xviii.

"Tame!" Yes: to one who believes the history was mere fiction, it may well be so. But that is begging the whole question.

Having inserted his sceptical wedge, however, he pretends to drive it in by "critical" arguments. "Accordingly," he says, "we find in it *plain traces* of the Elohistic writer." These 'traces' are two only;

i. The phrase, 'the cities of the circuit.' But why should that be thought "Elohistic?" *Solely*, because it occurs in xiii. 12ª, *which is part of a " Jehovistic" chapter;* and which was rent out of its context *solely on the assumption that* xix. 29 *was " Elohistic."* A vicious circle.

But this is not all. A moment's reflection would have shewn that in xiii. 12 the words "cities of the circuit" naturally presuppose the occurrence of some defining phrase, such as "circuit *of the Jordan*," in *vv*. 10, 11: so that *v*. 12 cannot be torn away from *vv*. 10, 11.

Observe, too, that the phrase "cities of the circuit" occurs in xix. 17, 25, 28; proving (*ex hypothesi criticorum*) that it is a "Jehovistic" phrase.

It is clear, then, that if we are to apply induction to the matter, the inference is, that the phrase belongs to J; for it is found only in "Jehovistic" chapters.

ii. The clause, "God remembered Abraham." Yet this exactly falls in with the supposition that *v*. 29 is part of the whole narrative xviii, xix.—Abraham's intercession for the cities appeared to have been utterly in vain. But it was not so. "God *remembered Abraham*," and heard that yearning prayer which his heart had offered, though his lips had not expressed, for Lot's deliverance.

As this passage xix. 29 is a stock instance with the Disintegrators, let me add a critical remark, which is quite decisive as to the inseparability of *vv*. 28 and 29. The verse begins "And it came to pass, when . . . ." Now this is a *continuative* way of speaking, introducing some new circumstances connected with what has gone before. See Gen. iv. 8. xxxv. 17, 18, 22. Numb. x. 35. Cp. Gen. xxiv. 30.

CHAPTER V.

Consideration of two specially strong cases, pointed to by Dr. Colenso, as irreconcileable with Unity of Authorship.

1. THE remarks made in the preceding chapters have shewn the fallaciousness of the method pursued with so much self-complacency by the "Critics." There are few of the alleged cases of variation of "style," which are not explained by what has been already said.

One or two instances, however, look, in Dr. Colenso's statement, so curious, that it may be worth while to notice them separately.

2. One of these relates to the pronouns אֲנִי, אָנֹכִי. "Who can suppose," he says, (p. 2,) "that one and the same writer would have employed in X אנכי [m] *fifty-four* times, and אני *thirty* times, and in E have reversed the proportions, and used אני *seven* times (= *twenty-four* times in X) and אנכי [m] only once [n]."

(*a*) Now I will not spend any time here in inquiring, whether this be a more valid test than the use of ἐγώ and ἔγωγε would be in Plato. It is, of course, not probable that the "Analyst," who in four consecutive pages mis-spells the word אנכי four times, would care for the nicer delicacies of language. To him the terms are hard "formulæ," like $f(x)$ and $f(y)$. But he can scarcely refuse to be accessible to the following argument:—

---

[m] I have omitted the points; (see above, 36). K.

[n] Why suppress the correlative, "= *three* in X"?—I only call attention to this as shewing the *animus* that pervades every, the slightest, detail. K.

(b) In chap. xxvii, which Hupfeld and he "give wholly" to the "Jehovist," (C. A., p. 130,) אָנֹכִי occurs *seven* times, (that is, *as often as in the whole of the Elohistic document*) and אָנֹכִי NOT ONCE.

Can any more complete refutation, not only of the argument founded on this particular word, but of the whole of this most "*un*critical" method, be well imagined?

3. But another case remains, which he has reserved for the climax of his argumentative display. "It is *still more inconceivable*," says Dr. Colenso, "that the little particle of entreaty נָא could have been used by the *same* writer *eight* times in each of xviii and xxiv, *nine* times in xix, and *seventy-four* times in X altogether, and *not at all* in E; not even in xxiii, where Abraham throughout uses forms of courteous entreaty, yet never uses this particle." (p. 27.) And again; "E *never* uses נָא, but he has instead of it לֹּי in a formula of entreaty, xxiii. 5, 13, 14." (p. 25.)

The answer to the argument founded on this grand, insoluble, difficulty is very easy.

(a) Chaps. xx, xxi are repeatedly affirmed to be in all respects similar "in style" to the chapters, which are assigned to J. Yet there is no instance of נָא in them.

Either, then, the non-occurrence of the particle is of no consequence; or these chapters must be taken away from X.

This is ample reply to the "Critics;" but for men who wish to go a little deeper into the matter, we add:

(b) The absence of נָא from the parts assigned to E, can excite no surprise, when we consider their *contents*. Ch. i is an account of the Creation; there was no room for it there. Nor do we look for it in the genealogies, which occupy a large fraction of E. Nor in the account of the Covenants made with Noah and Abraham. Nor in the patch-work tacked on by the Disintegrators to these main chapters. Indeed throughout the portions denominated "Elohistic" there is not one instance where the particle of *friendly entreaty* would be in place.

CHAP. V.] *The effect of the particle* לִי *in* Gen. xxiii. 55

As regards ch. xxiii, the Analyst's remark only shews that he has neither perceived the different effect of the two particles, nor understood the position which Abraham occupies in that chapter. Abraham is not using the language of *friendly entreaty:* the whole transaction rests on another basis. He maintains throughout a *dignified* courtesy. He respectfully, but decidedly, declines the overtures of Ephron. He wished to *purchase* publicly (not to receive as a *gift*,) a burying-place in the land which God had made over to him in reversion. And the Hittite chieftains address him in a corresponding way. They call him "a prince of God:" "*Hear us, my lord: thou art a prince of God among us.*" All is stately and grave and (in the good sense) diplomatic; and the use of the formal and weighty לִי° is in exact keeping with the general character of the chapter.

So easy to be conceived is Dr. Colenso's "inconceivable." It only requires that we should view language as the instrument of human thought and feeling,—not as a set of algebraic formulæ.

° Cp. Ewald, *Ausf. LB. d. Hebr. Spr.*, 329 b. "Eigentliches *Wünschwörtchen* ist das stärkere *Bedingungs*wörtchen לִי."

SECTION III.

THE REAL NATURE OF THE PRETENDED "ANALYSIS," VIEWED IN ITS PRINCIPLES, ITS METHOD, AND ITS RESULTS.

" C'est là une critique fort commode, émanée plutôt d'une certaine coquetterie sceptique, que du desir de chercher et de connaître la vérité."

M. MUNK, (Lecon d'ouverture).

CHAPTER I.

**The Principles on which the Disintegration-theory rests;
—(1) Religious Unbelief; (2) Historical Pyrrhonism.**

1. WE have seen that the two Criteria, which are supposed to be employed by the "critics," fail to supply any ground for the disintegration of Genesis.

Here, then, we might stop. The adverse evidence has been sifted, and proved to be valueless. Truth resumes her old position;—only the more honoured, for having passed safely through this fresh assault, and come out of it *sans reproche*.

2. *Argumentatively* we might do this; and if it had been simply a matter of scientific interest that we had been discussing, one would have been content to proceed no further.

But this is a matter of vitally *practical* importance; in which the highest interests of mankind are involved.

In such a case it is well not only to *refute* error, but to trace it up to its causes, and explain, so far as may be, the *nature* of its mistakes. This is what we propose to do, very briefly, in the present chapter.

3. I. *First*, then; the ultimate ground of the dismemberment-theory is *Religious Unbelief*.

The question of the authenticity of the book was, evidently, decided long before the "Critical Analysis" was set on foot. The muster-roll of phrases has no more real office to fulfil than had the senate of Tiberius or the jury of Judge Jeffries. Unbelief—the spirit that refuses to recognise any Divine intervention in the world's history—had already settled the matter.

If Genesis be an authentic document, then it is certain that there is an *objective* basis for Religious Faith. God *has* communed with man. Preparation is thus made for the future introduction of Christianity. The Gospel has its roots buried deep in the world's history:—for its seed was laid in the Protevangelium, (Gen. iii. 15). To get rid of this book of Genesis, then, is a necessary preliminary for any assault on Christianity. When that has been effected, there may be some possibility of carrying out the theory of modern Unbelief by founding a religion on INTUITION [a].

4. Setting out from this stand-point, the "critics" *assume* that no such supernatural communications as those recorded in Genesis could have taken place. That is, they *assume* the very point which it was incumbent upon them to *prove*, if they are to escape the charge of being guided by wilful, unreasoning, unbelief.

The essence of Revealed Religion lies in the fact that the Creator of the Universe is also the Friend of Man,—the "God of the spirits of all flesh,"—the "Saviour of all men, and specially of them that believe." This condescending love of God, which is imprinted on every part of the Bible, (though it was fully revealed only in and by our Lord Jesus Christ,) has its first, strong and marked, exhibitions in the book of Genesis. As we read it, the exclamation, "What is man that Thou *so* regardest him!" perpetually rises to our lips. "See the *philanthropy* of the Lord!" (ὅρα τὴν φιλανθρωπίαν τοῦ Δεσπότου,) is the constantly recurring remark of St. Chrysostom in his Homilies on this book.

Unbelief resolves, that all these manifestations of God's kindness to His human children shall be considered *impossible*. The "eternal Power and Godhead[b]" are held by it to be irreconcileable with the "Divine philanthropy[c]." The First Chapter of Genesis is thought to present "much *more correct views* of the nature of the Divine Being" than the narrative

---

[a] "I know in what I have believed," said Strauss; "a *subjective*, not an objective, Christ."
What is this but *Anti-Christ*,—a rival Christ of man's own creating?
[b] Rom. i. 20.   [c] Tit. iii. 4.

in ii. 4—25, (p. 37); because the latter passage has "very strong, anthropomorphic expressions, ascribing human actions, passions, and affections to the Deity." (p. 36.) All this is prior to any "critical" inquiry. It is a foregone conclusion.

5. Again: it is *assumed* that the chapters, in which so many traces of *man's sin* are recorded, are not true;—that they could not have been written by any but a gloomy, sombre-minded, and (it is frequently insinuated) impure writer; (p. 39—41).—Certainly, such narratives are not what WE should *wish* to have inserted in our Sacred Books. Man would rather hide his deformity, or gloss it over with the charms of poetry and romance. But the Divine Physician means to lay bare the festering sore, with the view of bringing the sick to apply to Him for help. *This* is what Scepticism refuses to tolerate.

An eminent statesman has lately said [d]; "There is one history, and that *the most touching and profound of all*, for which we should search in vain through the pages of the classics,—I mean, *the history of the human soul in its relations with its Maker*—the history of *its sin and grief and death, and of the way of its recovery to hope and life and to enduring joy.*"

This great history is to the Rationalist an impertinence, a scandal. It cannot be true. It shall be assumed to be a fiction. Retain, if you please, the memory of Creation's being "very good";—but cut out the account of man's Fall. Erase the record (mercifully brief as it is) of all that brought the Sin-Flood on the Earth, or that led to the destruction of the Cities of the Plain: and let us have none of the deep spiritual history of Abraham or Jacob. The details of the two Covenants, the account of the Purchase of Machpelah, the Genealogies, and various mutilated fragments,—these may be left;—for no one will readily think that a document

---

[d] Mr. Gladstone's *Address at Edinburgh*, Nov. 3, 1865.

made up simply of these came from the hand of the great Lawgiver of Israel [e].

6. Similarly, it is *assumed* that no such thing as prophetic *prediction* is possible.

Jacob foretold that Ephraim should take precedence of Manasseh. *Therefore* ch. xlviii must have been written about the time of Gideon, at the earliest; (p. 74—76. 109, 110).

It was foretold to Rebekah that the elder of her sons should serve the younger. This must be "considered as contemporary history," (p. 98,) written 800 years after the birth of Jacob.

Jacob's Blessing "is regarded, like the other predictions, as a *vaticinium ex eventu*, a piece of historical narrative, referring to facts contemporary with the writer [f]." (p. 121.)

One cannot help wondering, why, if this simple argument were also correct, such a precarious process as that of the "Critical Analysis" should ever have been resorted to. But then Unbelief has found, that many, who can readily perceive the grossness of the *petitio principii* in the case just referred to, are unable to detect it when it is wrapped up amidst the endless convolutions of a pretended "Criticism."

---

[e] Dr. Colenso utters strange insinuations against the writer of those parts of Genesis which he has omitted from the interstices of his "Elohistic" fragments;—as if one who *recorded* the sin of man, *created* it. Yet it remains certain, that the most necessary preliminary for a right understanding of human history is the recognition of SIN in man; and that the only account of the origin of man's fallen state is that which we find in the Book of Genesis side by side with promises of his eventual recovery.

"That man only," says Schlegel, "who recognizes the whole magnitude of the power permitted (under the inscrutable decrees of God) to the wicked principle, . . . is capable of understanding the phenomena of universal history." (*Phil. of History*, Lect. xv.)

[f] Thus scepticism, at least, bears witness to the exactness of the correspondence between the prophecy and the event. Sometimes it does more;—bringing out into vivid clearness points which commentaries have left unnoticed. E.g. Dr. Colenso calls attention (*C. A.*, p. 249) to the strangeness of the fact that Jacob should have given Shechem to Joseph, "*Jacob being now a poor dependent in Egypt*, and the land in question [being] in Canaan."—A very noticeable circumstance this, undoubtedly.

7. II. *Secondly;* These main positions of religious scepticism are supported by a thorough *Historical Pyrrhonism.*

The facts of history cannot be demonstrated *à priori.* There is always a *possibility* that any event *might* have happened otherwise than it is related to have happened.—Therefore it is always *possible*, in the abstract, to *doubt* whether a given history be true.

There have been minds to whom the *possibility* of doubting seems to have become converted into a *habit* of doubting.

And this habit of doubting is mostly followed by recklessness of assertion. The field of actual history having been swept clear of *facts*, why should not the void be filled with *conjectures*,—which to the dreamer are far dearer than facts? Why should not history, as well as theology, be made to rest on a man's own *intuition?*

Thus, in either direction, (at the will of the pyrrhonist,) "A posse ad esse *valet* consequentia."—'*That* MAY be false; I reject it.—*This* MAY be true; I assert it.'

Such cases of inability to appreciate historical evidence, when they are produced by no moral obliquity, are among the most singular in the whole range of mental pathology.

8. One of the best-known instances of this historical pyrrhonism is supplied by the Jesuit Father, Hardouin; whose writings exhibit many resemblances to the extravagant doubts and no less extravagant conjectures of the modern pseudo-critics [g].

E.g. In his "Chronologie expliquée par les Medailles," P. Hardouin maintained that the whole ancient history of Greece and Rome was written in the xiii[th] or xiv[th] century; —the only genuine Greek authors being Homer and Herodotus; the only genuine Latin writings being those of Cicero

---

[g] Indeed it is probable that there is an actual historical connexion between the two. Hardouin was only one of several Jesuits, who at the end of the seventeenth century endeavoured to destroy the credibility of documentary and historical evidence; and in so doing prepared the way for Voltaire and his school; who in their turn gave the main impetus to the development of unbelief in Germany.

and Pliny, with the Georgics of Virgil, and Satires and Epistles of Horace.

In another work [h] he affirmed that all the "Acts" of the Councils, up to those of Trent, were fictions. There never were any heresies, he maintained, prior to that of Wickliffe. Arianism, Manichœism, Pelagianism had no existence except in the so-called works of the Fathers; which, he asserted, were all forgeries, and full of heresy [i].

9. But on what grounds did he maintain such views?

The wilder any absurdity is, the harder, of course, it must be to give any consistent account of it. One or two instances of his mode of procedure may suffice for our present purpose.

(*a*) Often his assertions are made unhesitatingly without any pretence of reason. He, or a friend who told him, *knows* it [k].

(*b*) Often he thinks an insinuation of *bad motives* sufficient. E.g. The men of the xiv[th] century had heard of the great names of antiquity, and they resolved to publish their works under the protection of those names, "*quoniam id è re suâ erat*[l]."

(*c*) Sometimes it is STYLE on which he takes his stand. Thus *Thucydides* did not write the works that go under his name;—for, in fact, there are evident traces of *Gallicism* in them [m].

(*d*) Sometimes he erects a theory on the slightest possible ground, and then, when met by inconvenient facts, he calls in the help of "interpolators." Thus he had argued that Pliny was a native of Rome, (not, as commonly thought, of Verona,) *inasmuch as* he frequently says "nostræ urbis" of

---

[h] *Ad Censuram Vett. Scr. Prolegomena.*

[i] "Scripta illa, quæ Patrum vocantur, fomenta sunt hæresium omnium." (Ib., p. 223.)

[k] *Prolusio*, p. 60, 1. (quoted by Lacroze, *Vind. Vett. Scr.*)

[l] *Ad Censuram*, p. 178.

[m] E.g. In Bk. iv. we have οὐκ ἦλθον ἐς χεῖρας, for "they came not to close quarters;" which is bad Greek, clearly representing the French, "n'en vinrent pas aux mains."

Rome, but *never* calls himself a Veronese.—But then, (it is urged,) Pliny, in the Preface to his Work, calls Catullus of Verona his countryman. "Yes," he replies, "but the First Book of Pliny, which embraces the *Indexes* AND the Preface, is of no worth. The Preface *is a mere patch, stuck on by interpolators* [n], as is plain from *the immense difference of style* between it and the rest of the work;" (which difference is purely imaginary).

(*e*) Sometimes he determines, what *ought* to be historical fact, on *à priori* grounds, and derides the *absurdities* involved in the vulgar belief. Thus he points out how monstrous it is to suppose that Josephus, the Jew, should write about the History and Antiquities of Palestine *in Greek;*—or that he would reckon time by *Olympiads*,—"much," he says, "as if a Spanish writer should date his years from the Hejira."

(*f*) Sometimes he acts the part of a severely accurate historian [o], refusing to believe a well-attested fact *because some other authority does not mention it*. Thus Julius Cæsar, he maintains, *never conquered Gaul;*—it is an absurd fiction, *contradicted by the* COINS. "His victories in the *East* are well substantiated by his *coins;—we have nothing of the kind about Gaul*[p]."

(*g*) He indulges in bold statements, which are afterwards softened down into harmless and irrelevant propositions. Thus after arguing that Ælfric's (Anglo-Saxon) *Homily on the Eucharist* is not genuine, because it is written in the character called Anglo-Saxon, (which was the invention of the "fourteenth-century men,") he adds, "AT ANY RATE, the characters are different from those used by King Offa on his coins; which are *undoubtedly* Roman [q]." Besides, he adds,

---

[n] "Esse quippe pannum subdititium, attextum ab interpolatoribus, vel una styli in Præfatione incredibilis a reliquo opere dissimilitudo admonet."

[o] His brother Jesuits, putting on the like air, affected to call P. Hardouin "*le plus rigide des Critiques.*" (Lacroze, p. 65.)

[p] *Chronol. Vet. Test.*, p. 235 (quoted by Lacroze.)

[q] Cp. Lacroze, p. 34: "Le P. Gennon pretend que toutes ces piéces *sont*

the *name* ÆLFRIC looks like a fiction: probably being only from the Hebrew אל and פרק; " whom God redeems ʳ."

10. None who have examined the works of the modern " Critics," from whom Dr. Colenso has drawn his materials, can fail to recognize how precisely their mode of historical procedure corresponds to that of the Jesuit Father. There is the same unlimited freedom of doubt, the same unrestricted licence of conjecture, the same paralysis of the historical sense.

Let me add a few specimens.

(*a*) I take the first from Dr. Colenso's translation of "Kuenen *On the Pentateuch.*" The author—an advanced freethinker—had written; "If for the present we leave out of consideration in our inquiry THE DECALOGUE, *about whose high antiquity scarcely any doubt is entertained*," . . . .

Dr. Colenso prints the last words thus: "Scarcely any doubt [?] is entertained." Kuenen was quite correct in his assertion ˢ; but, of course, pyrrhonism *can*, if it will, lodge an unanswerable objection against him;—how is it possible to reply to a note of interrogation? It is a universal sol-

---

fausses, ou DU MOINS *suspectes:*" (everything, in fact, being in his argument "suspect," which is not absolutely beyond the possibility of doubt.)

ʳ This etymological artifice (the easiest and paltriest of all) is a favourite with the sceptics. A little before Hardouin's time, J. P. Speeth (afterwards called Moses German) maintained that Philo's works were written in France; and that his name was nothing more than the French *filou*, (" pickpocket.")

Some of the latest instances of this puerility are found in Dr. Colenso's Translation of Dr. Oort's " Worship of Baalim." Dr. Dozy derives the Arabic "*gorhum*" from גרים, " sojourners;" and the name of the Mekkan idol, *Hobal*, from בעל. I find it—I must avow—quite impossible to believe that Dr. Dozy is not making experiment on the gullibility of the " Critics." It is inconceivable that any good Oriental scholar should *believe* in the validity of such intensely absurd etymologies. One might just as well assert that M. Thiers is of Irish origin, because his name is clearly capable of being 'analyzed' into " The Erse."

ˢ Dean Milman remarks, (Jewish Hist., i. p. 132), "As to great part of the Law in Exodus, Leviticus, and Numbers, *most of the boldest writers*, Eichhorn, De Wette, Ewald, Bunsen, Bleek, admit that it is of the age, if not from the lips or the pen, of Moses."

vent, if a man can bring himself to use it with sufficient freedom from scruple.

One cannot gather from Dr. Colenso's work, what his notion of the venerable Lawgiver of Israel was; or why he is so unwilling to concede him that lofty position, which the rest of the world have with one consent assigned to him. Let us hear Dean Milman's statement[t]. "Such was the end," he says, "of the Jewish Lawgiver,—a man who, *considered merely in a historical light,* without any reference to his divine inspiration, *has exercised a more extensive and permanent influence over the destinies of his own nation and mankind at large than any other individual recorded in the annals of the world.* ... Throughout Europe, with all its American descendants, —the larger part of Asia, and the north of Africa—the opinions, the usages, the civil as well as religious ordinances, retain deep and indelible traces of their descent from the Hebrew polity."

Yet Dr. Colenso is still in doubt, who this Moses was;— what he did;—what he wrote;—what he believed. "Truly herein is a marvellous thing."

The Israelitic Church thanked God through many centuries for the illuminating, comforting power of the Law given by Moses;—it had "opened their eyes;"—and "YE know not whence he is!"

(*b*) Dr. Colenso is constantly insinuating, sometimes openly imputing, dishonest motives to *his* writers of Genesis;—one of them being (as he *conjectures*) the pure and saintly *Samuel. E.g.* The repeated mention of Hebron in Genesis was, *he conjectures,* to help David in making Hebron his political capital. "It *seems probable* that with a view to this the passages before us were written[u]." Just as *probable,* as that

---

[t] J. H., i. p. 213.

[u] p. 81. Two pages later Dr. Colenso writes somewhat more modestly: "He MAY have advised him to make Hebron the seat of his government, and MAY have written the passages before us with a view to that event." But also he MAY have been (I, for one, am sure he was,) utterly incapable of such an act.

F 2

such a dishonest endeavour should have had the effect of winning to Hebron so great honour, that, after 3,000 years, the city is to this day called *El-Khalil*,—" The Friend,"— and Abraham's tomb there is visited in this nineteenth century, with real and deep interest, by a Prince of Wales !

I am not willing to offend the reader and pain myself by giving more instances of this kind. I would only add, that Dr. Colenso's theory compels him at every step to impute intentional deceit to the authors of *his* Documents;—deceit, too, relating to the highest matters, involving them in the guilt of pretending that "the Lord had spoken, when the Lord had not spoken." Is this view *probable?* If not, if it be in the highest degree *im*probable, if it rests (as it does) solely on gratuitous conjecture, what are we to think of the state of *his* mind, who can fill a thick volume with the flimsiest *pretences* to reasoning, all of which from the outset assume the truth of this hypothesis?

(c) He finds in the details of Noah's Ark and the Mosaic Tabernacle "indications of artistic skill of every kind; *which can scarcely have existed in Israel before the age of Solomon*[x]," &c.

Why not?—Dean Milman says[y]: "I have a strong opinion that at the time of the Exodus the Israelites, at least their leaders, were *in a higher state of civilization* in many respects than at any period of their history before the Captivity excepting perhaps during the later reign of David, and that of Solomon[z]."

---

[x] p. 96. Cp. 73: "We find in the Elohist no mention of *houses;*"—and the argument implies that this arose from there *being* no houses in the time of the "Elohist," *i.e.* according to Dr. Colenso in the time of Samuel!

[y] Hist. of the Jews, p. 135.

[z] Cp. also p. 144. "*All the difficulties,* which were urged by the objectors, and which embarrassed the asserters of the truth of the Mosaic history, with regard to the attainments of the Jews in arts, in skill of workmanship, in mechanical processes, *have been swept away by the recent discoveries* of the progress of the Egyptians in all these signs of civilization. . . . Of everything mentioned in the books of Exodus or Leviticus, the pattern or the process may be seen in the volumes of Sir G. Wilkinson, Rosellini, or Lepsius."

(*d*) Jacob in his "Blessing" couples together Levi and Simeon. This Dr. Colenso considers to be " one of the *most decisive proofs* of the low condition of the Levites in the early part of David's reign." He adds: "It seems absolutely impossible that any one . . . *living after the age of Moses*, should have expressed himself thus about the Levites, *if* the books of Leviticus and Numbers had been in existence in his time and their laws in operation *to any extent*."—As if any unprejudiced person thought of asserting that Genesis xlix was written "after the time of Moses." —Hear again what Dean Milman says[a]: "These two families [Simeon and Levi] are condemned to the *same* inferior and degraded lot, as divided and scattered among their brethren. Yet how different their fate! The tribe of Levi attained the highest rank among their brethren; scattered indeed they were, but in stations of the first distinction; while the tribe of Simeon dwindled into insignificance, and became almost extinct. *A later poet, certainly Moses himself, would not have united these two tribes* under the same destiny."

(*e*) Dr. Colenso in maintaining that the holy Name, *Yahveh*, is of post-Mosaic origin, is at once confronted with the difficulty that the name of Moses's mother is beyond all doubt a compound of that Name.

How does he meet this fact?

By simple PYRRHONISM. The argument, he says, (p. 273,) is "based mainly, if not wholly, on the assumption that the name 'Jochebed' WAS *really* the name of the mother of Moses."

The only *reasons* which he can think of for justifying his doubts are, (1) that the name "Jochebed" is not mentioned

"All this most minute detail concerning the construction of the tabernacle which fills many pages in the book of Exodus, must surely be contemporaneous. . . . What could induce a writer, or even a compiler, to dwell on it with such extraordinary detail at a later period?"

[a] J. H. i. p. 63.

in Exodus ii; so that, he says, (p. 274,) "*it seems plain* that the writer of this part of the narrative *did not know* her name; and *it can scarcely be doubted* that E. vi. 20, xxvi. 59 [b], where the name 'Jochebed' is given to her, *are* INTERPOLATIONS."—This needs no comment.—(2) "AT ANY RATE," (he says,) this name, "Jochebed," cannot stand against the inference drawn from Exod. vi. 2—7;—an inference which has been shewn above to be completely valueless.

These are the grounds on which he discards a plain historical fact, accepted undoubtingly by so free a speculator as Ewald, (p. 272, 3);—who adds that "the name 'Jahveh' was no doubt in use already in the pre-Mosaic time;" and that "*BEYOND ALL DOUBT Moses made use of this Name in announcing* his revelation [c]." 'Beyond all *doubt;*'—but not beyond contradiction from *pyrrhonism;* which has not sufficient belief in Truth to entertain even a *real and serious doubt.*

(*f*) In *C. A.*, p. 242, quarrelling with a certain argument of Böhmer, Dr. Colenso writes: "*This assumes* that the accounts here given are accurate and true accounts of Egyptian matters, WHICH IS BY NO MEANS CERTAIN." It is not certain *à priori;* just as it is not *à priori* certain that the Saxons invaded England;—but none, who have taken pains to examine into the matter, have any doubt of it. Dean Milman says: "The information we obtain from the Mosaic narrative concerning the state and constitution of Egypt during this period, is both *valuable in itself* and *agrees strictly with all the knowledge* which we acquire from other sources [d]."

---

[b] So Dr. Colenso.—He, no doubt, means Numb. xxvi. 59.

[c] The candid reader may ask; "*How can* any one get over such evidence of the early existence of the name as is supplied, e.g., by Judges ii. 11—13. iii. 5—7. x. 6: 'they forsook YAHVEH, the God of their Fathers?'"

To the pyrrhonist there is no such thing as evidence. He has no one fixed point, except his own caprice. Says Dr. Colenso: "The above passages *appear to be interpolations* by a later hand." How is it possible to *reason* on such terms?

[d] H. of J., i. p. 51. Similarly of the book of Exodus he says (p. xxvii.):

Let any one, after reviewing the above specimens (which I have selected not as being the *worst*, but as being *instructive*, instances) of Dr. Colenso's mode of dealing with his subject, say whether the temper of mind, which they indicate, be not directly *anti-historical*.

Yet here (if anywhere) is the key-stone of his argument.

APPENDIX ON DR. COLENSO'S TRANSLATION OF 'OORT ON BAAL-WORSHIP.'

1. The following extracts from Dr. Oort's pamphlet will illustrate the character of Dr. Colenso's views of historical reasoning.

2. In his Part v, Dr. Colenso has devoted fourteen pages of close print to giving an account of what is either a sorry jest or else a grotesquely *anti-historical theory* of Dr. Dozy's, about some Simeonites having migrated a thousand years before Christ to Mekka.

Dr. Oort (p. 2) after commending Dr. Dozy's "results" as "likely to throw light upon the darkest questions," especially those which relate to the "original Israelitish worship," remarks, that such fresh light was *much needed;* the authors of the Books from which we have hitherto derived our knowledge, having "given us, *either in good faith or of set purpose*, a distorted image of it. *One after another, Prophets, Priests, and Rabbis,* regarding the history of ancient times from their own point of view, *have done their best to hide from us the truth.*"

Is this not a plain *reductio ad absurdum?*—Does Dr. Colenso not feel the irony?—' *Choose* one of the two.—Reject the evidence supplied by a few ridiculously incorrect etymologies (put forth by Dr. Dozy, " either in good faith or of set purpose"); or, believe that the writers of the holiest books in the world,—believe that the authors of Deuteronomy and the Psalms and Isaiah and Malachi— meant to blind after-ages as to a fact, with which they themselves were well acquainted, namely, the prevalence of Satyr-worship in the time of Samuel and David!—Of the two choose one.'

" Among the most remarkable points in the record in Exodus is *the intimate and familiar knowledge of Egypt. All the allusions*, with which it teems, to the polity, laws, usages, manners, productions, arts, to the whole Egyptian life, with which we have lately become so well acquainted, ARE MINUTELY AND UNERRINGLY TRUE."

Who but a pyrrhonist,—one who is totally colour-blind as regards True and False,—could hesitate for a moment?

Again: at pp. 3—5, Dr. Oort writes: "The Israelitish worship at Mecca has *not had the same development* [as that *in Judea*]. THERE were no Prophets, Priests, or Rabbis, who *thought it necessary, in the interest of their own convictions*, to set forth incorrectly the ancient state of things. Hence *there is ground for hoping* that at *Mecca* facts may be brought to light, in reference to the ancient religious worship of Israel, the traces of which may have wholly or nearly disappeared in the books of the Old Testament. . . . . . The religion of the Simeonites at Mecca *existed for about* FIFTEEN CENTURIES, *amidst constant vicissitudes, before we have any account of it.* . . . . MEN EASILY FIND WHAT THEY WISH TO FIND: MANY SHARP-WITTED SCHOLARS ARE THUS OFTEN LED UPON A FALSE PATH."

Dr. Colenso seems absolutely insensible to the irony of all this.

3. Dr. Colenso says in his Preface that between Dr. Oort and himself there is "SUBSTANTIAL AGREEMENT." Now at pp. 18, 19, Dr. Oort says: "*The whole Old Testament agrees in this*, that after the deliverance out of Egypt, in the wilderness of Sinai, a Covenant was made between JHVH and Israel; *in other words*, that JHVH *was then adopted as the national God of Israel.*"

This, then, according to Dr. Colenso, is but *slightly* different from his own views;—to which, in fact, it is fundamentally opposed.

If this be not historical pyrrhonism,—utter inability to discern the nature of Truth and Falsehood,—what is?

4. In his PART V, Dr. Colenso has occupied 16 pages with a translation from Movers's "Phœnicians."

Let us hear Dr. Oort's opinion of Movers: (p. 36). "Appeal is made for the contrary to Movers: *and there is some wisdom in this*,—since *out of his work may be proved WHATEVER ONE WISHES TO PROVE*. On this point he is altogether at variance with himself." And again (in reference to Movers; p. 35). "In point of fact, *the proposition is a mere* CASTLE IN THE AIR." And again (p. 37): "He (Movers) *asserts . . . He produces no proof for all this.*"

This, at least, is plain and sober truth. But then, what are we to think of Dr. Colenso, who in the course of a few weeks puts forth such contradictory positions;—now producing Movers as his chosen authority, before whose dictum the best established truths must recede and be abashed; *now* publishing to the world the opinion of his equally revered friend Oort that "by means of Movers *anything* may be proved?"

Is this the conduct of one who *cares for* TRUTH? or is it the recklessness of a pyrrhonist, who does not believe in the existence of such a thing as truth, but, while "flinging around him firebrands, arrows, and death, says, Am I not in sport?"

CHAPTER II.

On the METHOD by which the 'Critics' support their foregone conclusions:—including (1) Imaginary Cancellings; (2) Lacunæ; (3) Charges of Inadvertence, &c.; (4) Extreme Subdivision of chapters and verses; (5) Arbitrary Assertions.

WE have seen already in former chapters the illogical, uncritical, unhistorical character of this method. But we have a yet heavier charge to add. Whenever other means of evasion fail, the "Critics" habitually resort to suppositions of a writer's having *meant to cancel* something which *is* in the text; having written something which *is not* in the text; having been guilty of over-sight, inadvertence, and even plain self-contradiction. They cut up a single verse into two or more fragments. If this be found insufficient, then—any arbitrary fancy whatever is resorted to as proof.

All this is a clear confession that the Book, *as it stands*, CANNOT be disintegrated.

I.

Cancellings.

1. At p. 184, Dr. Colenso says:—

"The Jehovist, then, *as we suppose*, MAY have thought it best to *cancel* the whole of the insertions in these two chapters, xx, xxi, (except xxi. 6, 7 and the short link xxi. 1, which *was still needed*, in consequence of his own *long interpolation* in xviii, xix, to connect xxi. 2 with the previous Elohistic matter in xvii,) and to substitute for the matter contained in them the following : . . . . *By the above supposition we get rid at once of the difficulties* in (57)."

Again at p. 187:—

"The Jehovist, having thus *provided for* the derivation of the two names 'Bethel' and 'Israel' by means of two striking incidents, MAY *have intended to cancel altogether* the Elohistic passage, xxxv. 9—15, *and with it* also the Elohistic Section xlviii. 3—7, which *makes direct reference to it* e."

2. So far *his suppositions:* but now what are the FACTS? At p. 187 we read:

"*In both* the above instances, however, the older passages *have been still retained* in the text, ... *through some accident, which cannot now be fully explained.*"

Dr. Colenso seems never to lose his self-complacency under the most serious difficulties.

In *C. A.,* p. 124, 5, he writes:

"*On our view* the matter may be explained thus. In the document (EE$_2$) which J had in his hands, containing the original Elohistic narrative with the additions of E$_2$,—(that is, *as we suppose*, with the additions of J himself at an earlier period of his literary labour,)—stood the passages xx. 1—17. xxi. 22—27ª, 32. xxvi. 18. The Jehovist MAY *first* have merely inserted the verse xx. 18, and filled up xxi. 27^b—31. *Then, on again revising* the story at a later day, he MAY have seen that there was hardly anything said about *Isaac*, . . . and he MAY *have thought it best to* CANCEL the passages xx. 1—18. xxi. 22—34 *altogether*, and write a similar narrative for the earlier part of *Abraham's* life, with the substitution of 'Pharaoh' and 'Egypt' for 'Abimelech' and 'Gerar,'—such a narrative, in fact, as now stands in xii. 10—20. . . . . He MAY then have written the passage xxvi. 1—3, 6—11. . . . He MAY then have *filled up* the story of Isaac with xxvi. 12—17, 19—25, and *added v.* 26 —33 *to supply the cancelled passage* xxi. 22—32. Finally, he MAY have inserted *also* a passage xvi. 4—14. . . . .

"Thus," he adds, "*the whole may be* EASILY AND INTELLIGIBLY EXPLAINED."

Of the *ease* with which such explanations may be manufactured, there can be no doubt. The *rationale* of Dr. Colenso's process is simply this:—

---

* Cp. pp. 226. 235. 250. 255. 259. 260. 266: and *C. A.,* 89. 138.

If the *facts* of the case are against him, *tant pis pour les faits;*—they shall be altered.

Lord Bacon in a well-known passage has advised us to *torture* facts by thoughtful and reverential study of them; the new Criticism saves itself the trouble of thinking by irreverently *distorting* facts. "Viam aut inveniam *aut faciam,*" is its motto.

Such measures may, indeed, serve the "Critic's" purpose of "getting rid of difficulties,"—in his own book. But reflecting men will know what inference to draw from this facility in violating the sanctity of documentary evidence.

3. One more instance: *C. A.,* p. 138:

"*We suppose, as before,* that he *intended to cancel* the original story of E in xxxv. 9—15, BUT *let it stand as it was* for a season, *perhaps from a wish to reconsider it.*"

Can aught go beyond the miserable grotesqueness of this last suggestion?—as if three thousand years ago, one of "the great and good men, leading men of their age," (Dr. Colenso, p. 180,) when writing a book for the use of the "schools of the prophets," had exercised all the cautious *indeterminateness* of the "Critical" Analysts;—who, after seventy years of perpetual re-adjustments of their scheme [f], are still afraid to commit themselves to any positive system, lest some inconvenient fact should forthwith spring up to overthrow it [g].

---

[f] Ilgen's "*Urkunden*" was published in 1798. Hupfeld (quoted in *C. A.,* p. 154, 5) speaks of it as written "in the first wild period of criticism, *with colossal arbitrariness and violence;*" yet he confesses that "the greater portion" of his own supposed discoveries are found in Ilgen. No marvel;—if, indeed, like causes produce like effects.

[g] Cp. *C. A.,* p. 80. "At last he (*i.e.* J) *may* have interpolated other episodes .... and in these he *may* have employed almost exclusively the name 'Jehovah.' BUT *we must reserve this point for further consideration.*"

The same trait is observable in Hardouin. E. g. "Quorsum autem prisci illi scriptores ... nobis veniant in suspicionem, *tutum est in aliud tempus referre.*"

Every new move in the "Critical" *game* brings a new piece on the board: and so it is necessary to be wary and to have a very long memory.

II.

Lacunæ.

Moreover various *lacunæ* (such is the cruel exigency of Theory) must be supposed to exist. Passages once in the Document have now disappeared,—except to the eye of the toiling " critic;" whose vision is so quickened by desire, that " absens ut præsens sit," and the non-existent becomes to him a vivid reality.

1. Thus Dr. Colenso writes ;—

" Here then, *according to our view*, occurs the first blank in the Elohistic story, *i.e.* WE MISS the account of Jacob's reaching Padan-Aram, of his receiving his two wives," &c. (*C. A.*, p. 152.)

" Something *appears to be missing* here from E." (p. 161.)

" The E link, describing how these ' Midianites ' *became possessed* of Joseph, has been *lost*." (p. 206 : cp. 215.)

2. In all these cases, however, (as if to add to the critic's annoyance,) the difficulty ceases the moment we take the book of Genesis as *one* document. There is then *no* lacuna ; —all is clear, harmonious, and complete.

Such are the trials that " critical " genius has to endure ; —it must not only pant and toil beneath its heavy burden, but must *appear* to the lookers-on to have imposed the burden on itself gratuitously.

III.

Charges of inadvertence, &c.

Again :—to maintain his hypothesis, (compared with which duty everything else in the " Critic's " eyes becomes insignificant,) he must charge the writers, whom he himself has bidden to start into existence, with *inadvertence, carelessness, waywardness*, and other faults.

—So the Pagan, after creating an idol, has been known to revile, and even to scourge it, because it did not fulfil his desires.—

1. This is often done in terms of arrogant disrespect.

In *C. A.*, p. 14, Dr. Colenso quotes and " agrees with"

Hupfeld's remark, that the Compiler " *has just written down here at once what came to his pen.*"

Yes, Sir; it is very true; "the Compiler" *is* capable of doing what you have charged him with;—for he is simply the creature of your own brain; and may *be* and *do* what you *will*. But please to remember what follows from this; he is the counterpart of your*self*; the free and easy remarks you make of him must most surely come back upon you. "DE TE fabula narratur." The short-comings of the "Compiler" are wholly yours. He is but your automaton. It is *you* that " write down at once what comes to your pen."

2. So, too, Dr. Colenso says (*C. A.*, p. 16) of another of *his* writers, that he " is here merely exercising his fancy upon " an etymology.

Again: *C. A.*, p. 81. " He MAY have written, ' from thence,' *loosely*, ... *merely to introduce his own interpolation*." (Cp. p. 62, and *C. A.*, p. 82.)

And; *C. A.*, p. 206: " He has *clumsily retained* the original words of E."

The "clumsiness" is, of course, wholly due to him who has produced it by attempting to sever the component parts of a living organic unity. Part the veins of a living body from the arteries, the nerves from the muscles, and then complain of your " results " looking clumsy!

IV.

Vivisection of Chapters and Verses.

Again:—to gain even the faintest appearance of coherency for his "documents," he is compelled to resort to extreme subdivision not of chapters merely but of one and the same verse. The mere complication of these details (apart from any thought of the Protean artifices by which they require to be supported) is no slight argument of the unreality of the whole method of procedure [h]. E. g.

---

[h] It may be necessary to explain that 12^a signifies the *first clause* of *v.* 12; 12^b the second clause; and so on.

1. Chap. vii is distributed thus (*C. A.*, pp. 22—29):
1—5 (J), 6—9 (E), 10 (J), 12^a (E), 12^b (J), 13—16^a (E), 16^b, 17 (J), 18^a (E), 18^b, 19^a (J), 19^b (E), 20 (J), 21, 22 (E), 23^a (J), 23^b, 24 (E).

2. The *first five vv.* of Ch. viii run thus (*C. A.*, p. 29):
1, 2^a (E), 2^b, 3^a (J), 3^b (E), 4^a (J), 4^b (E), 4^c (J), 5 (E).

3. The *first half* of Ch. xxx thus (*C. A.*, p. 152):
E has *v.* 1^a, 4^a, 5, 6^a, 7, 8^{ac}, 9—13, 17, 18^{ac}, 19, 20^{ac}, 21—24^a.
J has *v.* 1^b, 2, 3, 4^b, 6^b, 8^b, 14—16, 18^b, 20^b, 24^b.

This "Analysis" (self-refuted already [i]) is supported by five pages of writing, which might well be thought to have proceeded from some one who was ridiculing the whole scheme. (See especially p. 156.)

4. At p. 63 Dr. Colenso points out that Böhmer has fallen into "hopeless difficulties. His object," he says, "can only be effected by not unfrequently *breaking up* a single verse, in a very arbitrary manner, into *two*, or *three*, or even *four* fragments."

Yet Dr. Colenso effects *his* object only by breaking up *forty* verses of Genesis into *two* fragments apiece, *eight* into *three* fragments apiece, *six* into *four* fragments apiece, and one into five fragments [k].

V.

Arbitrary Assertions.

Lastly: Dr. Colenso is constantly employing mere *arbitrary assertions* as pretexts for dismemberment. I will detain the reader with only two out of countless instances.

---

[i] In Dr. Colenso's own words, (speaking of Böhmer:) "The above appears at first sight *exceedingly artificial*, and could not be received, unless supported by *strong internal evidence.*"

[k] If any one wishes to look further into this vertiginous subject, he may examine ch. xxi, xxv, xxix, xxxii, xxxvi, xli, &c.

1. In *C. A.*, p. 27, he has made up his mind that vii. 16—21 must be dissected in the following way :—

16ᵃ (E), 16ᵇ, 17 (J), 18ᵃ (E), 18ᵇ, 19ᵃ (J), 19ᵇ (E), 20 (J), 21 (E), (a complication which is at once self-condemnatory): and he gives, among other similar *reasons* for it, the following :—

"*v.* 20ᵇ; 'and the mountains were covered,' is Jehovistic; *since it would be a tame and spiritless repetition*, if written by E after *v.* 19ᵇ ; *e. g.*, 'and all the high mountains that were under all the heaven were covered.'"

2. Now, *first of all;* at p. 24 he had quoted Böhmer as saying, "When we consider the *diffuse* style of this writer (E), there is nothing to surprise us in such a repetition;" and again, at p. 97, he quotes Delitzsch thus : "It is *impossible to mistake here* the narrative style of the Elohist,—*diffuse, delighting in repetitions.*"—So that it is confessedly *in the manner* of the writer of the passages, which are assigned to E, to use repetitions.

3. But ; *secondly ;* if ever there was an occasion when the effect of such repetition was awefully and majestically solemn, surely it is this ;—when the writer is gazing in spirit on that Sin-deluge, and seeing the mountain-tops gradually disappear beneath the waves [1]. Those repetitions sound—not merely like the successive surgings of that irresistible tide, or as the recurring expressions of the historian's deep emotion, but rather—as the (all but audible) relentings of Divine Mercy, contemplating that most necessary work of Divine Justice.

4. In *C. A.*, p. 189, Dr. Colenso says :—

"It will be observed that xlviii. 7 makes no reference whatever to the *cause* and *circumstances* of Rachel's death, which as recorded in xxxv. 16—20 are so remarkable. *This seems to shew* that the two passages, as they now stand, cannot be due to the same author."

[1] Ewald, who with all his rationalism differs many degrees from the school to which Dr. Colenso has attached himself, observes that the *repetition* in Gen. i. 27 seems to express the *joyful emotion* with which the writer contemplated the wonderful fact he is narrating; "So God created man in His own image ; IN THE IMAGE OF GOD *created He him.*"

That is; Jacob, when speaking with Joseph, *could not allude* to the death and burial-place of Joseph's mother without at the same time giving a full account of the "cause and circumstances of her death;" though these must (one would think) have been familiarly known to Joseph.

Is this reasoning? or is it mere arbitrary assertion?

5. I must avow, that to me it seems to resemble nothing so much as the play of children, who in imitating the serious pursuits of their elders will employ, with great persistence, fictions which they have extemporised for the moment; making up for the slenderness of their artifice by an innocently wilful mock-gravity, which triumphs over any amount of the most transparent inconsistency.

But then,—when such trifling is deliberately applied by adult men to sacred things, how inexpressibly great must be the guilt [m]!

CHAPTER III.

The Results of the 'Analysis.'

After all the labour which the "Critics" have expended, —after all their ambiguous dichotomies, their bold manipulation of evidence, their vague conjectures, their cancellings, supplementings, and arbitrary assertions,—what is the quality of the results they have to present us with?

---

[m] As I have, throughout these pages, restrained my expression of feeling within the narrowest possible limits, let me beg the reader's attention to the following weighty censure, from the pen of Dean Milman, upon one who, compared with Prof. Hupfeld or Dr. Colenso, is a rational guide to Jewish History.

"This [his account of Deuteronomy] Ewald, with unusual modesty, admits is only *highly probable.* He assumes the composition of the book at this time with the same *peremptory, I had almost said, arrogant confidence,* as if he were writing of the composition of the Æneid in the time of Augustus, or of the Code and Pandects in the reign of Justinian. *Having carefully examined all his alleged reasons, I confess that I cannot discern the shadow of a sound or trustworthy reason even for conjecture.* To historical authority there is no pretence." (*History of the Jews,* i. p. 338.)

CHAP. III.] *What are the RESULTS of the 'Analysis.'* 81

This question need not engage us long. The avowed object of the disintegration-theory is (as we have seen[n]) to find something which might seem to countenance them in their resolve to deny to the book of Genesis all "historical" value. No marvel, then, if the results of the disintegration (supposing it to be effected) should be worthless, *dead*, fragments. *That* was the very thing aimed at.

The "Critics," who might (one thinks) at least have grieved over the (supposed) necessity for depriving the world of "the oldest and most venerable document of human history[o]," are eagerly bent on "securing" this object at all risks, and in the face of whatever difficulties [p].

Let us look, then, at the character of these (imagined) Documents, E and J, which are now to displace that unique book of Genesis. The PROCESS, by which they have been shaped, has been found faulty at every step; but it is *possible* that the results may have such simplicity, truthlikeness, and internal concinnity, as may make us accept them in spite of all.

Is this the case?

I.

The "Elohistic" Document.

1. The Book of Genesis, as it stands in the Hebrew, has a clear and orderly progression from first to last:—its parts adjusted with admirable symmetry and bound together by numberless links of language and history.

How is it, when we come to the Document E?

2. After having been disengaged from surrounding and closely adhering matter with the most lavish expenditure

---

[n] Above, p. 23. [o] Above, p. 27.

[p] Cp. p. 12: "No expenditure of time and labour which may be required for this purpose, will be deemed superfluous or ill-bestowed by any who *are practically acquainted with the difficulties of the case*, and who appreciate at the same time the very great importance of these researches *in their relation to some of the most momentous controversies* of the present day."

G

of means, it turns out to be the most incoherent and unintelligible of writings. Its parts have no proportion or harmony. It accounts for nothing: it leads to nothing. E.g.

3. At the end of the first fragment all that God had made is "*very good.*" Then the pedigree of the antediluvian patriarchs is inserted; and next, without any warning, all is *most evil.* For aught that has appeared, man had continued in his high estate, retaining the Divine "image." Enoch had "walked with God," and Noah had "walked with God." Yet all at once " the earth was corrupted before God, and the earth was filled with violence." What is never seen in any single individual *is* seen in the whole race;—the whole world "*repente fuit turpissimus.*"

4. Then the Deluge is sent;—again, without any warning. No gracious respite, no time for repentance, is allowed. Then a solemn promise is given that mankind shall not again be cut off by a flood. But in spite of the hope such a promise held out, *mankind* is at once lost sight of. No "blessing" is in store for the race. *Per saltum,* we are introduced to the ancestry of Abraham, and then told of his leaving his native land and migrating to Canaan.

5. *Why* he should have gone forth, to encounter what in early days was the severest of trials, residence in a foreign land [q], we know not. Nor is there anything in the rest of the document that throws any light on the point. He migrated, says Dr. Colenso, "*proprio motu,*" (*C. A.*, p. 47);— and that is all we know of the matter.

—So in the Democritean theory of the world's formation, the atoms coalesce into this endlessly wonderful Universe *proprio motu :*—an explanation by which nothing is explained; if it be not rather a provision for excluding the only rational explanation.—

---

[q] Delitzsch, in more than one of his writings, has noticed the fact that the German word for *misery*, *Elend*, originally meant "foreign land" (Eli-lend). I believe the etymology is undoubted. The feeling, which it indicates, was almost universal among ancient nations;—it is not extinct even in these days of easy international communication.

In the true " Genesis,"—the book that has a real " genetic" influence on both history and theology,—everything is intelligible even to a child. The simplest peasant understands why Abraham left his home. He was called forth by God, in order that " in and through him all the families of the earth might be blessed." The most uninstructed can follow the gradual discipline of Abraham's faith, till it reached that never-surpassed elevation in the Twenty-second Chapter.

There,—in the true 'Book of Origins,' the authentic Genesis,—all is clear, and full of deeply important meaning. *Here*, in the " Critic's" figment, all is obscure and purposeless. We know nothing of Abraham's motives or character, his trials or his faith. He is neither the 'Friend of God,' nor the 'Father of the Faithful.'

6. Even the few parts of the narrative, which are spared to us, follow each other without any organic connection:— many times with an abruptness which might (one thinks) have startled even a " Critic." E. g. One part of Document E is made to run thus:

" All the men of his house,—house-born or the purchase of silver, or of the son of a foreigner—*were circumcised with him*. And *it came to pass, when God destroyed the cities of the plain*, that God remembered Abraham, and sent forth Lot from the midst of the overthrow."

" The overthrow!"—a most signal interposition of the Divine Hand;—that left behind it, graven on the earth's surface, a record of which no Israelite could be ignorant; —which is alluded to in such marked terms by Moses (Deut. xxix. 23), by David (Ps. xi. 6), by Isaiah (i. 9, 10), and by our Blessed Lord Himself, (in words of awful moment to an age which has had the localities of the Dead Sea set so vividly before it as ours has; St. Matt. x. 14, 15) :—how came that overthrow to take place?

A Christian child knows. The " Elohistic" document, drawn up by Samuel or one of the prophets (Colenso, p.

180), knows not. In the case of the Deluge some faint rays of light did find their way in; but here all is obscure darkness.

7. The rest of the book is equally barren and disjointed. Let me produce one more specimen, from the history of Jacob.—(I give Dr. Colenso's 'critical' renderings; p. 209.)

"And Jacob dwelt in the land of his father's sojournings, in the land of Canaan. These are the generations of Jacob. Joseph, a son of seventeen years, was tending with his brethren among the flocks, and he was a lad with the sons of Bilhah and with the sons of Zilpah, his father's wives. And there passed by Midianites, merchantmen. And the Midianites sold him into Egypt, to Potiphar, an officer of Pharaoh, Captain of the Guard. And they took their cattle and their gain, which they had gotten in the land of Canaan, and they came to Egypt, Jacob and all his seed with him."

I am spared the pain of making any remarks on this passage by a note which Dr. Colenso has added upon the same page. Knowing how invidious the task is which I have been led to engage in, I should perhaps not have ventured to speak of his work quite so correctly and frankly as he himself has done. What he has said, assuredly, no way *exceeds* the truth.

"It would seem that *no part of the dramatic history of Joseph's* being sold into Egypt and of his adventures there, is from the hand of the Elohist. *Indeed, it would be strange* if this writer, who has given us so LITTLE out of Abraham's life, STILL LESS out of Jacob's, and SCARCELY ANYTHING out of Isaac's, should have expatiated at so great length in the history of Joseph. But *the analysis shows* that *no part of this narrative* belongs to him, except, *perhaps*, [xxxvii] *v.* 2ª. 28ª, 36; which we assign to him as above, though with some hesitation."

8. Does the reader think this the lowest depth of absurdity? He may well be excused for thinking so.—But we have not done yet;—there is a lower depth still within reach of "Critical" penetration. Dr. Colenso's theory leads

him, nay, compels him, to suppose that the writer, who put this meagre composition together, was known, in the days of David and Solomon, "to have merely written *a work of imagination,—devout, instructive, edifying.*" (p. 78.)

Such, reader, is the consistency between the professions and the doings of these vaunting "Critics." Such are the choice rewards that Rationalism has in reserve for her toiling servants.

Truly, "of the vine of Sodom is her vine;"—promising refreshment to the weary traveller, but bursting into dust upon his lips.

II.
The "Jehovistic" Document.

1. We have already seen, more than once, the multiform character of the (supposed) "non-Elohistic" matter in Genesis. It comprises not only J^1, J^2, J^3, J^4,—the four "sets" of additions, made at separate "ages," by the one and self-same person J, (who is also identical with the "*Second Elohist*"),—but also an addition, J_2, "due" to a *friend* of J, (whose "style," however, is widely distinct from that of J, —no traces of it occurring elsewhere in Genesis,) and also some supplementary portions, named D, which proceeded from a writer who lived at least 300 years after J.

2. What animated these anxious endeavours, on each occasion, to add new matter to what had previously been deemed satisfactory, does not appear. The final result, as it now stands, proves that the successive additions must have been made under the guidance of some uniform principle, or some unerring instinct; for although each separate "set of additions" is fragmentary, (as Dr. Colenso frequently and very justly urges against Hupfeld and Böhmer,) yet the whole book of Genesis has as great unity, *as if it had been written by one and the same author.* Those gaunt-looking fragments, which we found so unsatisfactory in Document E, seem—now that the gaps have been filled up—as if they had been *designed* from the first to receive just these insertions.

Certainly, if *economy of hypothesis* were to weigh with us, we should say, it is incomparably better at once to suppose that the whole book was planned from the outset by one and the same mind.

3. But simplicity of hypothesis is only a small part of the inducement that presses upon us. As the matter is left by "criticism," it is impossible to make out what should have urged the "Jehovistic" writers to undertake the task they did; or why they should have become "Jehovists" at all.

The "Critical" theory supposes that they wished to establish the use of a new Divine Name, YAHVEH [r], which had been studiously avoided by their predecessor the "Elohist."

Yet, says Dr. Colenso, (p. 301,) the Elohist (and not they) was the person who really *introduced* the name.

But why should either he or they *wish* to employ it?

Was it that Almighty God had made Himself known by that name?—*That* would indeed be reason enough for their loving *and venerating* it.

No; say the critics; the "Elohist" *asserts* indeed that this was the case. He makes Moses to have given a "report of his awful communications with God," (*C. A.*, p. 261,) in which communications God had said, "I am YAHVEH;" —BUT this was a mere fiction on the part of the Elohist.

Dr. Colenso admits that, if such a communication really occurred to Moses, it was "a fact of aweful meaning and tremendous consequences." Yet he sees nothing improbable in supposing that Samuel *fabricated* the account of so solemn a transaction.

Why, what motive could he have had for doing so?

Oh, says Bishop Colenso, the Elohist "cherished grand

---

[r] The very *structure* of the word is a protest against such a notion; for it is formed from a verb הוה, which had already ceased to be used in Mosaic times. In the Divine reference to the name (Exod. iii. 14) the common form אהיה is employed.

Ewald (as quoted by Dr. Colenso) admits that it belongs, like "all other simple Divine Names and words of more recondite meaning," to a "distant primeval time." (p. 273.)

CHAP. III.] *How a people's religion may be elevated.* 87

ideas of the nature and character of Jehovah," and "with all earnestness imparted them to his 'disciples;" (p. 301). So,—wishing to propagate the Name, he *invented* this account, and inserted it in a forged history of the nation,— in gross violation of the command, "Thou shalt not *take the name of* YAHVEH, *Thy God, in vain.*"

Oh marvellous theory!

But what was there in this *Name*, that should make Samuel incur so fearful a responsibility as this? What marvellous potency had this combination of letters, that it should appear (as Dr. Colenso thinks it did appear) to be a likely means for elevating the religion of the people? The Name, says Dr. Colenso, (pp. 278—300) [or, at least, a name which differed from it only dialectically [s]] was the Phœnicians' name for their SUN-GOD:—was known to Israel as such;—must have been so known to them, "soon after their entrance into Canaan."

So,—*that* made it a suitable instrument for inculcating a high, holy, spiritual religion on the Chosen People! Samuel, "to whom first, in the depths of his own soul, had been revealed the grand idea of the One Only True and Living God [t]," (p. 283,) thought that the name of the Phœnician sun-god was the best vehicle he could get for the communication and perpetuation of that "Divine gift;"— although he was well aware of " the sordid usage by which it was debased *in the idolatrous worship* of the heathen tribes of Canaan, and in that of the multitude of his own people;" (*ibid.*)

But this is not all. Samuel devised this use of the Name; —and, in the next age, Nathan or some other " great and good man" carried out the plan, and entered into it so en-

---

[s] Namely יַהְוֶה.—This word is wholly a fabrication of Movers. *There is not the slightest evidence that there ever was such a word.*

[t] If this *revelation* be a *fact*, where in the history of Samuel is there any trace of it? If it be not, what shall we say of such a falsification of history as this assertion involves?

thusiastically that he seems at last to have come to think that the Name *had really been known from the beginning.* " He may have supposed," says Dr. Colenso, (*C. A.*, p. 14,) "that the *name* 'Jehovah' *was known from the very first,* but that the *worship* of Jehovah did not begin till the days of Enos."

Just as if St. Paul had adopted the name Zeus at Corinth, or Jupiter at Rome, as the grand means of propagating the truths of Christianity; and then in the next age Ignatius or Clement had come to hold the opinion that David had worshipped Zeus, or Jupiter.

After reviewing such a tissue of audacious, irreverent, and incongruous assertions, it seems an offence to Truth merely to say that the "Jehovistic" *Hypothesis* advocated by Dr. Colenso has not the slightest *prima facie* evidence to stand upon.—It is wholly and purely chimerical,—a fantastic midsummer-night's dream.

4. Let us, however, look for a few moments at the so-called 'Jehovistic' *Document;* and, avoiding all minor matters[u], attend to the one fundamental contradiction which is involved in the "Critical" theory about it.

That the "Jehovist," wishing either to inculcate a new Divine Name, or to reform Israelitic religion by means of an old polytheistic name, might, instead of composing an entirely new and independent work, have carefully retained a former Document, E, in which there was a laboured abstinence from the use of that Name;—that he should have done this at the cost of hampering himself throughout his book with minute endeavours to preserve consistency of details

---

[u] Such as the charge Dr. Colenso urges against *his* "Jehovist" (*C. A.*, p. 14): "The Jehovist, as we shall see, was not *very careful to avoid contradictions;*" (every such supposed contradiction being in fact a protest against the "Critical" Theory;)—or the contempt with which Dr. Colenso cannot help regarding his own fictitious authors: e. g. (*C. A.*, p. 18) "The whole story seems to us to be manifestly *due to the mere imagination* of the writer;"—that writer (D) himself being merely the *projection* of Dr. Colenso's own mind.—*Ipsi displicet auctori.*

between himself and the older writer:—all this, however strange, may to some minds, possibly, seem not incredible.

But go one step further,—and Dr. Colenso's hypothesis is seen to involve the "Jehovistic" writer in one huge, palpable, ever-recurring,—incredible,—self-contradiction [x].

The original document (according to Dr. Colenso) had stated that the sacred name YAHVEH was first revealed to Moses; and it had *rigidly* conformed itself to this view, nowhere employing that Name. The "Jehovist" from the first writes as if the name had been known to the earliest progenitors of mankind. One revision after another takes place,—writers "of very different ages" take it in hand,— but this contradiction is allowed to remain. The "Jehovists," with all their punctilious regard for the "Elohist," nevertheless (the words are Dr. Colenso's) "*entirely stultified his purpose and contradicted his statement.*" (p. 71.)

Yet it is certain that these writers (supposing them to have existed at all) must have been men of very subtle ingenuity;—not throwing additional matter into the original document at random, but weaving their insertions into it with much care and foresight, so as to produce a strong appearance of unity in the final work. Very often, (according to the "Critics,") the new matter is so closely involved with the old that in order to eliminate it, single verses must be broken up into two, three, or four parts. Constantly (according to the "Critics") they refer to, or even imitate, what the "Elohist" had written. Sometimes they insert *anticipative* statements to *account for* obscure passages in a later part of E. Nay, in one case, we have a remarkable instance of their conforming the spelling of two names, throughout five chapters, to the requirements of a subsequent portion of the "Elohistic" narrative; for, up to the place

---

[x] Dr. Colenso says: "The *contradiction* stands out now *more distinct and palpable than ever, when we have the Elohistic story separated by itself*." (p. 70.) We have seen that the *true* Genesis is in complete harmony with Exod. vi. 3—8.

where Abraham and Sarah have their new names given (xvii. 5, 15), these writers invariably employ the names Abram and Sarai; thus guarding against any want of symmetry between the new and the old matter. This is all plain. But,—with all their care for consistency on *other* points,—in regard to that one subject to which their minds must have been most sensitively alive, that to which they owed their very *designation*, that which their writings were above all intended to illustrate,—the employment of the Divine Name,—they were so grossly negligent, that a "palpable" contradiction runs through the whole book.

Well may we marvel at the *credulity* of Unbelief!

CONCLUSION.

ONE, who was speaking from the stand-point of philosophical history, has said [a], "No poetry, no philosophy, no art, of Greece ever embraced, *in its most soaring and widest conceptions,* that simple law of love towards God and towards our neighbour, on which 'two commandments hang all the Law and the Prophets.'"

Who would not wish that a volume, in which so precious a treasure as this (to go no further than this) is contained, should be treated,—if not with loving affection,—at least, with respectful candour?

But when we proceed to examine "the Law and the Prophets" themselves, we feel how their claims on our veneration increase. Not only does that principle, which is the core of religious and moral life, *exist* in them; it was, moreover, preserved and guarded by them through ages of gross religious corruption.

How is this singular fact to be accounted for? How came that bright light to shine in the midst of surrounding darkness?

Bishop Colenso (with whom here at least we heartily agree) has remarked, (p. 300): "With such fearful practices and loathsome abominations prevailing among their people, (even in their most sacred places, 2 Kings xiv. 24, xxiii. 7,) the language of Isaiah and Jeremiah, breathing *the spirit of holy fear and trust and love,—of meek piety and patient faith,—of pure, self-sacrificing devotion to the cause of truth and righteousness*—presents a most wonderful and amazing contrast; and by that very contrast convinces us . . . . that they spoke God's Word to man, and taught Divine Truth as they were 'moved by the Holy Ghost.'"

[a] Mr. Gladstone's *Address*, (as above).

Most true. No other adequate account can be given of this phenomenon.

But then,—we cannot stop here. These prophets themselves supply the strongest conceivable evidence that what they were inspired to do was,—*not* to publish a true theology for the first time, but—to *recall* their countrymen to an old and well-recognised system of teaching which had been among them "from ancient times."

Isaiah begins, in his very first utterance, with a quotation from the Song of Moses (Deut. xxxii. 1); and throughout the chapter his complaint is that the people have *rebelled* against their Father and Lord. Jeremiah is full of references to the Pentateuch [b]. The drift of his prophesying to Israel (like that of Ezekiel's) is briefly this: "I brought you out of Egypt; I led you through the Desert; I gave you this good land; and you have defiled it with your idols. Therefore the land shall be spoiled, and I will plead with you in the wilderness of the nations."

This is all perfectly clear. In fact, we are better acquainted with the real course of national life in Israel, than we are with that of any other people,—our own not excepted.

The Historical books, the Psalms of David, and the Prophets are all in perfect harmony with the Pentateuch, *as it stands*. They give light to it, and it to them. The character of Jewish Faith, such as we know it to have been, is explained by the Pentateuch, and no other consistent account of it can be given [c].

---

[b] He, too, takes his commencement from Deut. xxxii. 1. See ch. ii. 12.

[c] The plausible statement, that the *Semitic race* was, by some natural peculiarity, monotheistic, is at variance with the plainest facts. This has been forcibly put by M. Munk, (who succeeded M. Rénan at the *Collége de France*,) in his Inaugural Address, Feb. 1, 1865.

"Le prétendu monothéisme des Sémites .... est tout un échafaudage de déductions philologiques, que le plus leger souffle suffit pour renverser. *Point de preuves historiques, point de critique serieuse basée sur des documents authentiques ;* au contraire, presque chaque page de la Bible et de nombreux passages

By the confession of Dr. Colenso himself, the First Book of the Pentateuch existed, very nearly as we have it, in the time of Solomon;—before the time of Homer. We know in general, well enough, what the religious state of the nations of the world was at that time,—what hold polytheism had already gained everywhere. How came such a book as Genesis, (a book which still supplies the most cultivated religious thought with much of its most valued material,) to exist then? or how came Solomon and David and Samuel to be what they were?

Admit the authenticity of the Pentateuch and all is solved. Deny it, and all is impenetrably dark. One of the most conspicuous facts of history, namely, the existence of a pure religion for fourteen centuries among a people not less naturally prone than the rest of the world to sensual idolatry, has *no* explanation. Other miracles, which affected the physical world for brief intervals of time, may be got rid of;—this enduring miracle in the sphere of spiritual life cannot.

Thus much as regards the general *à priori* view of the position occupied by the book of Genesis.

As to the so-called "critical" assaults on its authenticity, we have seen that there is nothing in them deserving of the

des auteurs profanes donnent à cette hypothèse le plus éclatant démenti. Car ce n'est qu'une hypothèse, une théorie établie *a priori* dans un certain but; et chaque fois qu'on a voulu l'appliquer, on a rencontré des exceptions. Les Sémites, a-t-on dit, étaient monothéistes. Mais les Assyriens? exception: les Babyloniens? exception: les Syriens et les Phéniciens? exception: *ce qui veut dire, que la race Sémitique était essentiellement monothéiste, excepté—tous les peuples Sémitiques.* 'Mais vous oubliez les Arabes,' me dira-t-on; 'leurs monuments ne sont ils pas là pour prouver leur foi en un seul Dieu?' Et quels monuments, je vous prie? Une série de noms propres péniblement ramassés dans des écrits relativement modernes, et interprétés avec une sagacité philologique, qui meritait, pour s'exercer, des sujets plus sérieux." (p. 13.)

"En un mot les Sémites étaient astrolâtres; ... les Indo-Européens adoraient toute la nature. Mais les uns et les autres confondaient la créature avec Dieu; ni les uns ni les autres n'ont pu s'élever jusqu'à l'idée d'une cause première absolue, unique, independante du monde, Créatrice. C'est là le vrai monothéisme, et ce monothéisme, dans l'antiquité, nous ne le trouvons que chez les Hébreux seuls." (p. 17.)

name;—they are uncritical, illogical, and anti-historical. They rely altogether on certain presumptions, (especially on one drawn from a misinterpretation of Exod. vi. 3—8,) which have been examined and found to be altogether untenable.

Thus—

It has been *resolved* by them, to consider the sacred names ELOHIM and YAHVEH to belong to different writers;—contrary to the evidence of the Book of Genesis itself, and to that of all later writers.

Resolved, that no author shall be supposed capable of writing on *different subjects;*—so that, e.g., an account of the Creation could not have been written by the person who wrote the history of Joseph; BECAUSE—*the same words are not used.*

Resolved, that the above difference of language shall be called a difference of '*style;'*—though it has nothing whatever to do with style.

Resolved, to fix upon certain words as 'Elohistic,' and then to rend out of all 'Jehovistic' sections every passage which contains those words, so as to "secure" it for the 'Elohist;' —a vicious circle which pervades the so-called "Critical Analysis" from beginning to end.

Resolved, to ASSUME, from the commencement of the 'Analysis,' that Genesis *is* made up of two documents, each of them a work of *fiction.*—What wonder if one who looks through a tinted glass sees things in other than their true colours?

Resolved, to over-rule all difficulties, which facts may place in the way of the "critical" theory, by supposing, *ad libitum*, the existence of *lacunæ*, where there are none,—of intended *cancellings*, where none occurred,—of *interpolations*, *inadvertencies*, "*clumsy*" and "*half-mechanical*" writing, and even *contradictions*. Reason would peremptorily forbid a resort to such measures;—this *pseudo-rationalistic* criticism[d] seems to revel in them.

Resolved, that no events, which would ruffle the smooth surface of *à priori* probability, shall ever be admitted to be historical;—though genuine history is full of such events.

Resolved, to consider a prophetic prediction to be impossible, and therefore to suppose that all prophecies must have been posterior to the event to which they refer.— A mere unreasoned assumption.

Resolved, to hold that any notion, however destitute of evidence, if only it be, in the way of abstract possibility, *conceivable*, shall be treated (under cover of the word MAY) as an admissible,—probable,—and, at last, natural,—premiss of our destructive argument.

Resolved, that at all events we will hold the book of Genesis to be *non-Mosaic*, and its contents to be unhistorical.

In these and the like Resolutions, not in logic or philology, lies the sole strength of (self-styled) Criticism.

In writing these remarks I have endeavoured to think only of Bp. Colenso's *book*, not of *him*. Throughout I have been anxious to *minimize* any expressions of surprise or disapprobation, which Truth required that I should not wholly erase. If, by God's blessing on what has been here, however imperfectly, written, he should be convinced of the untrustworthiness of his chosen guides, and return to listen afresh to the teaching of Him, who alone " has the words of Eternal Life,"—the highest aim of these pages will have been attained.

^d In reading the " critics" one is reminded of that couplet in Molière,

" Raisonner c'est l'emploi de toute ma maison ;
Et le raisonnement en bannit la raison."

Ecclesiam Tuam, Domine, benignus illustra; ut et gregis Tui proficiat ubique successus, et grati fiant Nomini Tuo, Te gubernante, Pastores: per Jesum Christum Salvatorem nostrum. Amen.

www.ingramcontent.com/pod-product-compliance
Lightning Source LLC
Chambersburg PA
CBHW020858160426
43192CB00007B/980